8-20-68

Meaningful Religious
Experiences for the
Bright or Gifted Child

Meaningful Religious

Experiences for the Bright or Gifted Child

HERBERT B. NEFF

ASSOCIATION PRESS

New York

72

Publisher's Stock Number: 1678
Library of Congress catalog card number: 68-17777
PRINTED IN THE UNITED STATES OF AMERICA

CONTENTS

FOREWORD

THE past decade has seen a tremendous increase in interest in the gifted child. This has been brought about by a variety of factors, not the least of which was the Russian leadership in the satellite field. The word *urgency* perhaps best describes the present concern for gifted children.

Almost exclusively the concern for gifted children has been directed toward the public school. Such questions as "What are the schools doing?" "Why are the schools not doing more for the gifted?" and "Why are the programs not different from what they are?" are too often heard. With almost the appeal of another educational fad, popular as well as educational journals are flooded with articles on educating the gifted child.

Nevertheless the result of all this interest in the gifted child has been increased and better school identification. That recognition of individual differences in the positive direction requires differentiated instructions is not generally accepted. Indeed, the gifted child has a better chance of being identified and being provided for in the schools today than he ever had before.

But the gifted child's total life is not school-centered. Indeed, there is even reason to believe that the gifted child, in particular, will acquire most of his knowledge from sources outside of the school. Far too little attention has been given to the out-of-school life of the gifted child for us to make any claim that gifted children are being adequately provided for.

In this timely and provocative book Professor Herbert Neff aptly discusses the role of the religious institution in the education of gifted children. Research studies of large groups of gifted children have repeatedly indicated the inadequacy of the traditional religious program for such children. Indications are clear that many gifted children turn away from organized religion because of the inconsistencies in doctrine, inadequacies of leaders, and the lack of acceptance of a philosophy of individual differences by religious education leaders.

The need for attention to the gifted child in the religious setting is very great. As is so clearly pointed out here, religious leaders and parents must follow many of the steps taken by school. Recognition of the need for special education for any area of exceptionality is of major importance. From the recognition of this need will come, first, identification and then more adequate provisions for the religious education of gifted children.

Mr. Neff clearly points the way. It is not likely that there will be complete agreement with him, but his major premise is that we must first of all recognize that something must be done. His philosophy is sound. This book tells us some of the things we may prefer not to hear, but if we are going to have well-rounded and well-adjusted gifted adults who are contributing members of our society, our churches, synagogues, and homes must provide more adequate religious education for gifted children.

Walter B. Barbe
Editor, *Highlights for Children*

PREFACE

THIS book will provide understanding and direction for all of those who have, or are preparing to have, any religious responsibility for bright or gifted children. This category will include parents, youth group leaders, scout leaders, camp counselors, and every religious educator and leader—for, whether they will it or not, every church or synagogue has its share of talented children for which it is responsible.

This book is also written because the gifted child is receiving attention everywhere—everywhere, that is, except in the *religious* setting of home, youth organization, camps, and in religious education. He has no program of religious education which will challenge him or meet his peculiar religious needs. His parents, counselors, pastor or rabbi, and teachers have neither the training nor the materials they need to guide him.

This conclusion is not a guess. It is the result of three comprehensive studies (described in some detail in Chapter 1) I have conducted concerning the relationship of the gifted child and his religious environment. In my first study of over two thousand Protestant churches of all denominations, only two were found who were attempting anything special for their gifted children. Yet this study and the two just concluded indicate beyond doubt that the religious needs of the gifted child are not being satisfied. The church and synagogue are losing most of their gifted children, and active religious interest ceases to be

9

a significant factor in his life by the time the gifted child enters college, if not before.

Many books and articles have been published about the gifted child and his problems and programs in the public schools, but very little indeed has been written to help the gifted child religiously. Yet he encounters many problems which are peculiar to any situation where he is concerned with religion or moral and spiritual values.

In any situation gifted children, by the very nature of their gifts and personality, face problems and frustrations peculiar to their giftedness. In the home and religious group this distinct nature, coupled with the disturbing ideas and pressures of our modern society and the customary approach to religion and moral and spiritual values, creates untold problems for most of these superior children. Unless gifted children are recognized and understood, their problems faced and handled with skill and affection, and their religious needs met creatively, most of them will be lost to their faith. Society, the religious institution, and the child all lose more than they are aware of, and that irreplaceably.

A few gifted children manage to survive their pernicious problems and develop into consecrated laymen or brilliant religious leaders. However, in every case investigated that turned out satisfactorily from a religious education viewpoint, without exception there were understanding and tolerant parents, an unusually inspiring and creative religious educator, a discerning and interested pastor or rabbi, or an extraordinarily challenging friend.

All gifted children have the same needs which other children have, but the greater the giftedness the greater the needs. In addition, talented and creative children have needs beyond those of the average child. As of now, neither the religious home, the church or synagogue, nor their related agencies are sufficiently meeting this special need of the bright or gifted child.

Herbert B. Neff

1

BURIED TALENT [1]

It was Friday afternoon. Two boys, Bill and Bob, had just finished their first weeks in special classes for gifted children in a junior high school near Cleveland. As they were walking home Bob was bubbling enthusiastically about his anticipated fun over the weekend.

Bill seemed unusually quiet. Suddenly he kicked a small stone across the street, and exploded, "I hate Fridays!"

No normal boy just up and says things like that, and Bob was properly surprised. "You're kidding!"

Bill replied by violently missing another pebble.

Bob's curiosity was now thoroughly aroused by this unorthodox behavior, so he urged: "Come on now, how come?"

"Ever since I can remember it's been church and Sunday school every Sunday. I hate it!" Once started, Bill's bitterness rushed out. "I can't win. All I do is get bawled out for daydreaming or for teasing the girls. My dad scolds me for not listening to the teacher. But we never talk about interesting things, the way we do in school. Well, maybe once in a while it could get interesting, but when I start to ask questions about things that bother me and don't seem to make sense, everybody looks at me as if something was wrong. So I just keep quiet most of the time. Someday I won't have to go to church school."

[1] Portions of this chapter appeared in the article "The Church is Embarrassed by Its Gifted Children" which appeared in *The Christian Herald,* March, 1962, and is used by permission.

11

After a pause he added, "Bob, do you like to go to church?"

Without hesitation Bob said, "Yes, I do. We usually talk about things that are interesting. Our teacher tries to get us going asking questions—just as we do in school. Last Sunday we were talking about Noah and the flood, and our Sunday school teacher showed us some pictures he took on his vacation of dinosaur bones some geologists found in sandstone they say is over twenty million years old. It sure was interesting."

"Wow!" was all that Bill could say.

Waste of Talent in Religious Groups

Is this an unusual conversation? Indeed it is. I have made and am making an extensive study of the gifted child in church and synagogue. In the first study of over two thousand Protestant churches in a large metropolitan area, only two churches were doing anything to meet the special needs of their talented youngsters. Bob attends one of these churches. He is unusually fortunate.

Bill's case is not so unusual. He is only one of the many bright and gifted children who are bored, frustrated, and troubled in the average church-school situation. My studies disclose that if Bill's parents or Sunday school teachers are aware of any problem at all it is that Bill is a troublemaker. In fact, most of those who work with Bill in church probably do not recognize him as being gifted.

During the first study project, telephone queries were made directly to the pastors and/or religious education directors of area churches. They were asked whether their churches were doing anything special to meet the needs of their gifted children.

The replies usually went something like these: "We have no gifted children in our church." "There are no geniuses in our church school." "We believe that the retarded and handicapped child needs more help than the bright child." "We lose mostly the uninterested troublemakers, not the really talented boys and girls."

My more recent study (1967) included Protestant churches across the country, parochial schools of the Roman Catholic church, and religious schools and synagogues of Judaism. Although nearly a thousand more institutions were added to my studies, no others were found which had any special concern or program for their gifted. And disturbingly, I discovered that one of the two churches I had found earlier with a special religious education program for their gifted had dropped this special emphasis. The church school superintendent who had initiated the program had moved.

According to the best information I can find, fewer than 20 per cent of the Roman Catholic parochial schools have any program for their gifted children. And what special consideration the gifted receive affects primarily the secular types of subject matter. Religious teaching remains basically unchanged.

Of the major religious groups, the Jewish faith is doing the most for their gifted, with approximately two times as many gifted children as other groups have to begin with. However, their teaching involves no special program of identification or methods. I talked to a number of leaders and rabbis of both Reformed and Orthodox Judaism. They are losing very few of their gifted (intellectuals) until college. Then a heavy loss occurs which is more severe for Orthodox Judaism than for the Reform group. The loss pattern found in Protestantism appears to be similar to that of Judaism except that the greatest loss takes place a few years later.

My study of Protestantism shows losses of their gifted beginning to occur early in adolescence and culminating during college. In Judaism the loss is low until they enter college. The closely-knit Jewish culture and the solidarity of the Jewish family appear to be deterrents until disrupted by the college experience.

No major religious faith appears to be meeting the religious needs of their youth. The result is the frustrated curiosity of a Bill who wants desperately to learn about God and His place in the creation of the world, the mysteries of the universe, and the purpose of life with all its contradictions and inconsistencies. So many things confuse and trouble him. He learns one thing in public school and another thing in church school or synagogue; many times they do not seem to add up. But Bill has learned by this time that it does not pay to ask too many disturbing questions. If you do you are a "queer" or a "troublemaker," and any boy in his right mind does not wish to be either.

Bill is not alone in these problems. Many leading authorities on gifted children insist that most bright and gifted children face such problems earlier and with more insistence than do average children. While many churches believe that spiritual awareness develops with puberty and set the chronological age of twelve as the optimum time for catechism and confirmation, educators of gifted children hold that spiritual awareness depends upon the *mental* age of the child. This means that gifted children are ready for deeper spiritual insights and understanding long before they are usually given such instruction.

But this is not the only problem Bill has with religion. He and all those like him have a wider curiosity and ask more searching questions than do other children. He really wants to know *why* as well as what. In addition he is more receptive to new ideas which he holds as true until he proves them false to his own satisfaction. Ideas that come to him through reading or school studies, even though they may tend to differ with what he has been taught at home or in Sunday school or in some other religious setting, are accepted, at least, tentatively. Serious questions fill his mind.

It does no good merely to tell him that the Bible or that religious authority says thus and so, or to show unhappiness because he asks disturbing questions, or to imply that he lacks faith because he has serious doubts and does not repudiate the new in favor of the old. Bill can no more help the way he reacts intellectually to new and conflicting ideas than he can help that he is gifted in the first place.

If the usual approach to Bill's problems is persisted in, one or more of several unfortunate consequences are bound to occur. He may completely reject religion along with its values, creeds and doctrines. He already acts as if he had, and my study shows that more than half of the gifted children in the average church school do just this. If for some reason this extreme is averted, he may nevertheless lose his respect for religious educators, pastor or rabbi, and parents. Tremendously persistent guilt feelings may grip him if he feels that he ought to be a "good believer" but cannot. He may feel socially rejected as one who cannot conform. Agnosticism or cynicism may become his dominant philosophy of life. He may pretend to believe what he cannot accept intellectually in order to be accepted by his religious group and to escape censure. Or he may try to close his mind to truth, thereby producing no end of conflict and anxiety. The average parent, pastor or rabbi, or religious educator might be surprised at how often one or more of these attitudes grow out of their dogmatic "lessons" with their Bills.

Moreover, highly intelligent children are observant. They notice illogical and contradictory relationships, and in particular any troublesome inconsistencies in the conduct of those in positions of responsibility and leadership. Dr. Leta Hollingworth and Dr. Harvey Zorbaugh, among other leading educators of gifted children, have observed that in such cases the gifted child tends toward negative suggestibility. He tends to reject everyone and everything concerned with inconsistent thinking and living. This often results in rebellion against authority, and he may become contentious and overly aggressive.

Where Are Future Leaders To Be Found?

Significantly, however, one of religion's most potent natural resources is its gifted children. From among them must come many of the leaders it needs. But there is little doubt that much of this irreplaceable resource is unknowingly being wasted through neglect. This heedless negligence is hard to understand, for at the same time gifted children are receiving attention everywhere except in the church.

Books, articles, public schools, colleges, and national leaders are giving increasing attention to the educational needs of bright or gifted children. We are realizing that the gifted child of today is the Isaac Newton, the Benjamin Franklin, the Albert Einstein, or the Martin Luther and Albert Schweitzer of tomorrow. There is little doubt that leadership in any worthwhile human endeavor comes from among superior children.

In the decade just past incredible scientific progress and amazing technological ingenuity has, for example, conquered polio and put men into space. But during the same period major crimes increased sixfold. The religious institution has always emphasized the importance of spiritual gifts and has stood on the major premise that man needs not only physical and intellectual development, but moral and spiritual development as well. Our survival as a nation may well depend more upon social know-how and spiritual ingenuity than upon dexterity in manipulating atoms or spaceships. Are we, by our disinterest and discouragement, driving away our potential moral leaders?

Today there is a disturbing need for more able leaders in Christian churches and in Judaism. Robert Reardon, president of Anderson College, said recently: "In the decade ahead our primary problem will be to find competent people to staff our pulpits and our classrooms." To illustrate this point: Lewis Terman in the 1920's made a pioneer and monumental study of 1,400 gifted children. On Strong's Interest Blank religion was at the top of the list. In his follow-up study of these children, about 10 per cent of the boys chose the ministry as a vocation when they grew up. Recently I conducted a study of about the same number of the brightest boys I could find. They were in the top 2 per cent of their graduating classes. At the bottom of their lists of vocational choices were the religious vocations— chosen by less than 1 per cent.

This change in little more than a generation indicates the trend away from religious interests, at least religious vocations, by gifted boys. Although several denominations are seeing an improvement in seminary enrollment, most of the Protestant churches, the Roman Catholics, and the Jewish groups are still having trouble finding young people to provide spiritual leadership.

"Sorry, Father, this is not for me." Such was the general reaction found by George W. Cornell in an Associated Press syndicated article which appeared in the Chattanooga *Post* March 30, 1967. This attitude is found generally among college undergraduates when discussing the possibility of entering the Roman Catholic priesthood. According to this report, interest in religious vocation is not only failing to keep up with normal attrition but constantly falling farther behind. The decay of interest is nationwide. Through the whole parochial education system the picture is dismal. Unless something unusual happens, the Roman Catholic Church will find itself in a disastrous situation.

My own research supports this view not only among the Roman Catholics, but among Protestants and Jews as well. There is a marked growth of secular interests and vocational pursuits. In talking with several outstanding rabbis in our larger cities, I find that they, too, are in dire straits in recruiting young men for the rabbinate and teachers for their religious schools. "We need far more than we can find," sadly commented a rabbi of a large synagogue and school.

Furthermore, seminary entrance examinations and undergraduate grade averages indicate that the most gifted and talented young men are not generally among those who enter seminaries today. Where will the applicants come from if religious institutions continue to lose many of their potential leaders, as our studies indicate?

Recent Research

To counteract this loss of interest and the loss of gifted children, and to upgrade the curriculum generally, several major denominations recently have revised their church school curriculum materials. To check on the effectiveness of these changes and to reevaluate the trend found in my earlier study, I have conducted another survey which is being concluded now. This latest research polled the related interest and activities of nearly five hundred college students, divided about equally between a church-related college in the "Bible Belt" and a large state university not so influenced by religious factors. Freshmen, juniors, and seniors were included. My rationale in choosing college students was twofold: first, the college campus is the best place to find large numbers of gifted persons who will be making the major contributions to society in the years to come; secondly, college students are adolescents and young adults— the age at which the greatest loss occurs to organized religion.

This group includes those in the age of rebellion and those who are old enough to be growing out of it. If the loss were simply the result of adolescent rebellious assertion of independence, one should observe an increase, however slight, in religious interest and a firming of faith in the older students.

What did I find?

1. Among the students of the church-related college about 98 per cent had attended church and church school regularly as children and preadolescents. Less than one-third of the university students were so interested.

2. By late adolescence, about 50 per cent of the entering freshmen of the church-related college students showed declining or complete loss of interest. In the state university about the same pattern was found for the one-third who were active and interested in religion as children.

3. At the junior and senior level the interest and attendance had fallen so that more than two-thirds of the church-related college students had lost or were losing active interest in their churches. But less than 5 per cent of the state university students were still actively interested in religion.

4. Concerning the new curriculum materials: among those from denominations who had revised their lesson content, and who also had attended church school classes more or less regularly, a surprising 80 per cent said they had not used the new materials, or said they didn't know whether they had or not. Of the remaining 20 per cent, 9 per cent said they found the new materials more interesting and helpful than the older lessons. The other 11 per cent said they found the new materials little or no more interesting and helpful. Most of the students—about 90 per cent of the church-related college and about 40 per cent of the state university students—were members of denominations who were using the new curriculum materials in their church schools.

5. When these students were asked what suggestions they had to make church school more interesting, about 92 per

cent of the entire sample said, "Better teachers." Of these about one-third added, "Lessons that are more applicable to life," and another third, "More discussion." The remaining 8 per cent recommended, "Lessons that are more applicable to life," but did not feel a need for better teachers. Interestingly and significantly, this 8 per cent came from among those few who as juniors and seniors were still quite actively interested in their religion.

6. When the students were asked who had helped them most with their religious beliefs, parents stood by far at the top of the list. This was followed, but not closely, by friends and teachers. Listed by only a few were pastors.

7. In explaining any change in their attitudes toward religion and the church, the juniors and seniors used such statements as: "I have a more realistic viewpoint." "I have become more liberal." "I was forced to attend Sunday school all my life; now that I am not under pressure, I don't go." "I once thought it was a sin not to attend church and Sunday school. I know now it isn't, so I don't go." "I was bored to death!"

Of course some stated dogmatically that they had not changed a whit. But not one used the excuse, "I am too busy." It is very difficult to arrive at percentages when there is considerable overlapping of attitudes, and in many cases there were several expressions of changed concepts and understandings. But in general the attitudes expressed a definite change from conservative or fundamentalist viewpoint to a much more liberal stand.

What are the conclusions?

1. The church is still losing most of its gifted children, even in the church-related college.

2. The new curriculum materials adopted by several major denominations are failing to interest the gifted student, at least at the adolescent and young adult level.

3. Most of these gifted young people feel the need for better teachers and teaching in the Sunday school.

4. Those who as college seniors and juniors are still actively

interested in religion apparently have good teachers, but feel the need for more practical, life-centered lessons.

What are the implications? Obviously, if the church wants to maintain a position of influence and leadership in our society, it will have to do more than it is now doing to challenge and hold its gifted children. This study reveals something long known in educational circles—it takes more than interesting materials or subject matter to stimulate learning and to hold the interest of students. The *teacher* is still the single most important factor in any learning situation. His (or her) attitude, skills, knowledge, and methods make or break a class.

Tradition Sanctions Special Training

The present neglect by the church of its gifted children is not in keeping with the best tradition of religion of any kind. If the Jewish child in ancient times showed great promise, he, like Paul, may have sat at the feet of a Gamaliel. Suleiman the Magnificent combed his Turkish Empire for the strongest, fairest and most intelligent boys for special education in the Mohammedan religion. In the early Christian Church and in the medieval Roman Catholic Church the talented boys were sought out.

An eminent Roman Catholic educator says we can still see the results of this selective process. In any representative group of American boys and girls one will always find Jewish children to average about 100 per cent more gifted children proportionally than the non-Jewish. Many theories have been offered in an attempt to explain this lopsided incidence of giftedness. This Catholic educator suggests that for centuries *their* gifted boys were drained off into a life of celibacy as priests and monks, while the talented Jewish boys were having large families as rabbis. Whether or not there is any real merit in this theory of selective breeding, it does illustrate religion's historic interest in gifted boys.

The early history of the Protestant church shows a more than usual interest in talented children. But in recent times the gifted child has been lost in the lockstep of mass education both inside and outside the church. Outside the church the stimulating search for giftedness is by now well underway. Inside the church, for the most part, we still sleep. Why?

First of all, there is the popularly held idea that "genius will out"—the gifted child can "light his own lamp and find his own path." We have come to believe almost as a doctrine that it is the person with only one talent rather than ten talents who is most likely to bury his abilities. This may well have been true in Jesus' day when only the bright child received educational attention. But today we seem to be convinced that it is neither democratic nor morally right to give one child more help than another. Children are lumped together in most religious education classes according to age or grade in public school, regardless of ability or previous religious training. When we add the popular but completely false caricature of the gifted child as a freak of nature, we can see why most religious groups fail to recognize him or his special needs.

Second, much teaching in religious education is the pouring out of information—like water dispensed from a sprinkling can over little jugs, with the hope that some will fall in. One suspects, too, that many religious leaders and teachers are afraid to stimulate too much thinking and too many questions. Usually creeds and dogmas are memorized like the names of states. Far too often honest doubt is regarded as a sin rather than the path to a secure faith personally resolved.

Not infrequently one finds an attitude that is expressed in some such comforting words as: "Young people will be young people, and they must 'sow their wild oats,' but they will get back to their faith when they get older." All of my studies indicate the contrary. If it ever was true, it is not true of today's gifted youth. Very few ever again return to be actively interested in religion once they have dropped out. Those few who do return usually find the extremely liberal groups more to their liking.

On top of all this is the comforting and tranquilizing belief that somehow God will accept our sincere but often carelessly prepared teaching, inadequate materials, and skimpy facilities, and then by some miracle make it all glorify Him and us.

Christians, to cover their shortcomings, sometimes take refuge in the words of Paul ". . . not many wise men after the flesh, not many noble, are called: But God hath chosen the foolish things of the world to confound the wise; and God hath chosen the weak things of the world to confound the things which are mighty" (I Cor. 1:26-27). But this certainly is no license to give God less than our best and indeed underlines what too consistently happens when other interests, competing for the gifted child, educate him away from God to the point that God is not able to use him. The tragedy is not, of course, that God uses the foolish to confound the wise, but that the wise so often are not usable—and in this day and age, sometimes with the connivance and neglect of the church!

Any parent, church-school teacher, pastor or rabbi can begin to help gifted children, using the advantage of earlier and greater interest in things religious. However, anyone who is interested in helping gifted children must learn to know them and understand them. Encourage talented children to ask questions and teach them to understand *why* as well as what. Be tactful and honest with them. Harry Emerson Fosdick tells about a bright boy who one day blurted out, "I don't believe in your old God." Dr. Fosdick casually replied, "Well now, suppose you tell me about this old God you don't believe in." He thus was able to lead the child to faith.

And, above all, live what you teach.

The goal should always be to help every child become the best possible person he can become, using to the best of his ability those talents with which God has blessed him. This includes the gifted child.

My studies of gifted children in the religious setting provided the startling discovery that in the two churches that have special religious education programs for their gifted children, the dropout rate for the classes affected is only about 10 per cent. The dropout rate for the average church school has often been estimated to be as high as 60 per cent. The low rate for these exceptional churches cannot be explained simply on the basis of the conservation of their gifted children. No church has that many bright boys and girls. Apparently, special concern for gifted children results in special concern for all children. The individual differences of children are recognized, and teaching is provided to satisfy their differing needs. It would not be inaccurate to say that an education program which helps gifted children will help all children.

2

WHAT IS GIFTEDNESS?

Wʜᴀᴛ ɪs giftedness? Nearly everyone, it seems, has his own conception of what constitutes giftedness in children.

The pastor of a large church in answer to queries about the gifted children in his congregation replied, "Gifted children? You mean children like that boy on television the other evening?" He referred to a popular family situation program in which the son was discovered to be a "genius." After considerable elation at first, and then much worry and flurry about the proper schools and education, the discovery was found to be a mistake. The tests had been improperly scored. The story closed with the parents profoundly thankful that their son was just a "normal boy" after all.

When I asked a director of religious education whether her church was doing anything special to help their gifted children, she replied, "No. We have no gifted boys or girls in our church, and I'm glad we do not. Geniuses are so queer and freakish. They would be a real problem in Sunday school."

A Sunday school superintendent described the "gifted" children in his church: "We have some children who work and study real hard both in our Sunday school and in public school. I suppose you might call them gifted. But we have no special program for them. I don't believe that they need one."

A bit more extreme was this response from the superintendent of a smaller church: "Gifted children? You mean the kids the other kids call 'brains'? What happens to them when they grow up? Don't they usually go crazy or something?"

24

A Wealth of Misinformation

These are not isolated instances of the popular misinformation and pathetic attitudes toward gifted children. Of course there are quite a number of pastors, rabbis, and church school directors who have a better idea of what we mean by giftedness in children, but the range of information, misinformation, and attitudes is disturbingly wide. There are a number of reasons why this is true.

For one thing, cartoons, comic strips, TV, jokes and cheap books paint the gifted child as an overbearing but weak and skinny child with an oversized head, wearing thick glasses, spouting polysyllabic words. Many people believe that this "child prodigy" and "genius" will soon burn out, become insane, or at least neurotic. If the gifted child is perceived as being somewhat normal in appearance, many think that he will prove to be a very unpleasant problem.

Less bizarre, but just as pernicious, is the picture of the gifted child as a persistent grind who, by hard work, is able to pull down good grades in school. Intense effort sometimes is equated with giftedness and no doubt received some credibility from the oft-quoted statement attributed to Thomas Edison: "Genius is 1 per cent inspiration and 99 per cent perspiration." This is not to say that many gifted children do not work hard and have a lot of drive, but mere high achievement alone is not a valid criterion of giftedness. Many highly gifted children are underachievers, while some average children are overachievers. In either case the children can be hurt by expectations not in keeping with their true ability. We are beginning to wonder whether moderately gifted children are not being hurt by expectations and methods of teaching which are based on highly gifted children. We can expect too much.

Some fear, stigma, and misinformation always surround anything which is different from the norm or what we are accustomed to. The whole problem is further complicated by the fact that no one knows what giftedness really is. Nor is there universal agreement on the definition of a gifted child. Nor, as a matter of fact, is there any such person as a typically gifted child. All gifted persons are unique, each with different gifts and unusual combinations of gifts. To compound further this problem is the fact that the gifted child does not often appear to the casual observer to be gifted. There is no easily observable characteristic which marks him as something very special. Even the trained specialist who knows well the identifying characteristics often has trouble making a valid appraisal merely by observation.

However, the picture is not as dark as it may appear at first. While there are many misconceptions and much that we do not know, we are learning. We may not know what giftedness really is, but we have discovered much about its manifestations, the ways in which it can be identified, and some effective methods of developing it to achieve a fuller realization of its potential.

As we learn to know and understand gifted children, the unfortunate attitudes and false pictures will gradually disappear and we will be better able to help them. Above all, may we never forget that gifted children are still children. However talented they may be, they need love, and they need patient guidance as expert as we can give them.

Attempted Descriptions

Although we are not really able to define giftedness, there are many terms used to describe gifted children—in fact, too many. Willard Abraham tells of a graduate student who began a search for descriptive definitions of gifted children. (It is in this sense only that we will define them.) After several weeks of careful research, he had found over one hundred "definitions" which varied all the way from synonymous to contradictory, and he had only begun to dig.

No matter how giftedness is defined, there will be some who agree and some who disagree. Nevertheless, there is coming to be general acceptance of these terms: children with high IQ's, the brightest, the talented, the rapid learners, the mentally advanced, the academically talented, superior children, exceptional children, child prodigies or geniuses. The term *exceptional children* usually includes handicapped children. While the designation *genius* or *child prodigy* may still be used occasionally to refer to children with exceptionally high degrees of giftedness, these terms are coming to be used less and less in literature about gifted children.

Giftedness is always used to describe a high innate capacity to learn and create. A child is born with his giftedness. And while a child may not be using his gift to capacity, nor realizing his innate potential, it is not something that can be raised or lowered, or increased or decreased, to any appreciable degree by training or education. A child either is gifted or he is not gifted. Several attempts have been made to prove that giftedness can be learned, or that intelligence quotients can be raised. Several books and articles have been published purporting to prove this possible. But such "proof" has never withstood careful investigation. It is true that in some instances the score on an intelligence test can be raised by intensive training in the type of information tested, but such improvement is only temporary.

Another factor that may seem to indicate that giftedness can be learned or intelligence raised may be due to a previous lack of education. Most of the tests used today are based upon the assumption that the child tested has had an average education and average cultural opportunities for a child of his age and that he reads well. If his education has been below par, or if he has been culturally deprived, he will score lower than his peers and intensive training will raise the score. But in most cases, discounting injury and illness, the IQ scores level out eventually. Innate giftedness and ability change very little in a lifetime, even less in middle and old age than many people have been led to believe.

To date there is no accurate way to test children for most special gifts, but we can test for the elusive quality called "creativity." Of this we shall say more later in this chapter, but as a general rule gifted children are also creative—if they have one kind of gift, they have many gifts. It is the exception rather than the rule that a few children have one special talent which may be unusually great.

In secular education children are tested for giftedness on the basis of their intelligence quotient, or IQ, which is derived from standardized tests designed for this purpose. It is not within the scope of this book to evaluate the commonly used IQ tests, but to explain briefly their use and methods. These tests are for the most part verbal in character; they test a child's ability to use language. Educational research has found an extremely high correlation between verbal ability and intelligence as it relates to academic achievement. Some tests include ability in mathematics, ability to reason, and mechanical comprehension. Most IQ tests are group tests in which the answers are marked or written.

Sometimes in special cases individual and oral tests are given which some believe to be more accurate than group tests, but training and more time are required to administer them. This makes such tests impractical for general use.

The gifted designation will vary from place to place. Some may start as low as 110 IQ or as high as 140. Perhaps 130 would be an average starting point. Tests given from ages five to nine are considered by most authorities as being the most valid. Of several different scores, all things being equal, the higher score is more valid than the lower or even an average score. The reasoning behind this says that a child cannot test higher than his intelligence, but many factors—illness, emotional upset, educational background, or distractions—may cause him to test lower. The factor of chance has been reduced by the design of the test to be so small as to be of no significant consequence.

Sometimes too much dependence is placed upon the scores of IQ tests. This is unfortunate. While intelligence and IQ scores tend to remain fairly constant throughout childhood, middle age, and even beyond, test results may vary considerably, particularly on the lower side. This is especially true for the highly gifted. Most group IQ tests are designed to make the most valid evaluation for the average and for those approximately within thirty points above or below the average. The range of test items is usually not sufficient to measure adequately intelligence above or below these points. At best an IQ test is only an indication— one indication—which should be used with other indicators and factors. Actually, the IQ test measures only one kind of giftedness, the ability to learn the subjects taught in school, and gives no indication of some other more specialized kinds of gifts.

An outstanding illustration of this last point is the case of the currently popular writer J. D. Salinger. His giftedness as measured by IQ tests taken in school was nothing extraordinary, but his success as a writer indicates an unusually high ability to handle language effectively. Many similar instances are known.

A good definition of the gifted child is that which has been adopted by the American Association for Gifted Children. It states that *the gifted person is one whose performance in any worthwhile human endeavor is consistently remarkable*. Merle Sumption of the University of Illinois defines the gifted as *those who possess a superior central nervous system characterized by the potential to perform tasks requiring a comparatively high degree of intellectual abstraction or creative imagination or both*.

The first definition allows for actual achievement in any area, while the latter considers the potential to achieve. Perhaps the best definition would combine both aspects, and might go something like this: *The gifted person is one whose performance, or potential to perform, in worthwhile human endeavors requiring a comparatively high degree of intellectual abstraction and/or creative imagination is consistently remarkable.*

What Is Creativity?

It is true, but probably an oversimplification, to say that creativity is a quality of mind and attitude which causes an individual to produce something new, to think new thoughts, or to approach old thoughts in new ways, or to do something different. It is a willingness—with something of a drive—to turn the mind loose, to let the imagination soar, to break away from conformity, to accept risk and chance in a considered choice, to be curious and eager about new worlds of mind and space for exploration or change.

The truly creative thinker may, or may not, make a new mechanical device, or paint a strange picture, or write an inspiring book, or compose a stirring march, or find a potent antibiotic, or experience new religious insights, or find better ways of dealing with people. He may merely find the world an exciting place, with challenges and opportunities for service no one else sees as he does.

This creativity—or as it is sometimes called, creative thinking—is usually a function of high intelligence. Sometimes it is treated as if it were a thing apart from high intellectual capacity. Several studies, of which one by Getzels and Jackson is outstanding, seem to have differentiated two groups of gifted, the creatively gifted and the academically gifted. The effect of this division often results in thinking that if a person has one gift, he does not have the other. Usually these two functions of intelligence go together.

The factor which makes the apparent difference is evidently not so much a difference in ability as it is in interest. The highly creative child is also intellectually gifted, but may have lost interest in academic pursuits due to many possible causes, such as little challenge in school or brightness which is penalized. On the other hand, some persons who seem to be highly gifted in academic talents may not show high creative ability. Torrance and others, including myself, believe that this is the logical reaction to an education program that has served to stifle and squelch the tendency to think creatively; the compensation is highly conforming academic achievement.

The observable identifying characteristics of the intellectually gifted who are also creative will be considered more at length in the next chapter, but it can be said here that people who have creative ability have active imaginations and more often than not are nonconformists. This often gets them into trouble. Especially is this true of creative children. There really is no end to the kinds of things creativity can produce, nor, seemingly, to the irritations a creative person can inflict on the more conforming conventionalists of his group.

While the academically talented, or intellectually gifted, child is often thought of as strange or as a "brain" who may be a nuisance, the creative child is usually considered a dangerous misfit and troublemaker. Paul Torrance of the University of Georgia states that in all his studies he has failed to find a group in which there was not clear evidence of pressure against the creative members of the group.

Unfortunately, these high-ability people do not fit into the conventional academic mold, nor do they fit the popular religious pattern. We are not talking about the unproductive nonconformist, or the merely rebellious person. We are concerned about the frustrated and unchallenged child with high creative ability. Even more than the conventionally or academically gifted child, these children are disinterested troublemakers in the religious group and problem children making low grades in school.

We do not wish to give the impression that creativity is different from what we call giftedness. Actually, it is a kind of giftedness with certain characteristics that differentiate it from the ability usually evaluated by intelligence tests. Because of merely average grades these highly talented children will probably be rejected by the best colleges. Even if they are admitted, they no doubt will be further frustrated by the courses required of them. In the religious setting they merely drop out along the way and are missed scarcely more than a toothache that has stopped hurting.

On the brighter side is the fact that creativity is coming to be recognized as one of the most neglected areas of giftedness, yet it is one of the most important. Obviously, the need for new ideas, products, and new ways of doing things is essential to the progressive society. Moreover, we are discovering now that creativity is basic to success in many common occupations formerly not associated with creative thinking. Some recent investigations have revealed that sales people in department stores who are outstandingly high in selling make significantly higher scores in tests measuring creative ability. We are finding that creativity is important in occupations which seem to be quite routine. Certainly, it is an essential ingredient in any vocation that requires thinking for one's self, taking a different viewpoint, and using one's imagination in solving problems.

In the field of religion more ability is needed than the facility to feed doctrines, dogmas, and morals into the minds of children. What kinds of questions do they ask? Do they learn to think problems through? Are they becoming resourceful and responsible members of the religious community? Do they believe their own ideas to be of value? Can they give their imaginations some play, correlate facts with experience, and then correlate both with traditional dogma, finally coming up with some new insight or original viewpoint? Or do they learn to mouth well the same old truths? Paul and Martin Luther were creative thinkers. What kind of thinkers are our children becoming?

While creativity is beginning to get attention from educators and psychologists, little has been done yet to discover the quality in children and even less to develop it. It is neither discovered nor evaluated by the commonly used methods of testing. Dr. Torrance states that in all his studies he has not been able to find a counselor or psychologist who bothers to obtain a measurement of creativity in the children or adults in his care. As a matter of fact, most people do not know there now are quite accurate and sensitive tests available to measure creative thinking.

The correlation between intelligence and creativity is strong until one passes about 130-140 IQ. While there is some positive correlation between very high IQ's and creativity, that correlation seems not nearly as high as it has been commonly assumed. Torrance states that about 70 per cent of potentially creative children remain undiscovered by our presently used methods of testing.

Traditional tests of giftedness are heavily loaded with tests of skills requiring memory, recognition, comprehension, and reasoning. They do an excellent job of predicting achievement in school, but they do nothing to evaluate or predict possible success in creative thinking.

Schools, homes, religious groups, and mental health institutions are deeply concerned about the mental and emotional health of individuals. They work together in an attempt to achieve a healthy and well-rounded personality. But there is little question that the stifling of creativity erodes the very tendrils of self-satisfaction and self-realization. This stifling creates frustration and tension, and perhaps brings about ultimately a breakdown. The ability to think creatively is one of the most valuable resources a person has for meeting life's problems. Yet, more is done in home, school, and religious settings to frustrate it than to develop it. May we soon come to realize that of all his abilities man comes closest to God in his creativity. May we see, too, that there is little creativity in conformity.

Other Talents

Many, indeed, are the gifts God gives to man! Not only are there gifts which help one to learn, think, and create, but there is the gift of performance—an ability to do something far better than average. This is not to say that one who has this talent is not gifted intellectually or creatively. There may be an overlapping. More often than not, those who have one gift have nine more, so to speak. On the other hand, the range of gifts is wide, with many degrees and combinations. However, every person is unique, and every person has at least one gift.

A partial list of talents might include these: art, music (both performing and composing), leading and dealing with people, politics, sports, manual dexterity, strength, mechanical understanding, dramatics, teaching, research, collecting, curiosity, concern for others, writing, homemaking, spiritual understanding, administration, and helpfulness.

What we too often forget is that every special ability or gift requires special attention and opportunity to develop into a worthwhile and self-satisfying talent. We too often assume that talents and genius "will out"; if the ability is there, we say, it cannot be stifled. This is pure fantasy and poppycock. It may be true of some individuals in some instances, but more talents are buried than are developed and used. Giftedness of whatever sort needs discovery, training, encouragement, and opportunity for expression, or it may die unnoticed.

What is giftedness? Perhaps more than anything it is a tiny seed like that of the giant sequoia. At first almost microscopic in size, yet when given water, sunlight, and fertile soil it grows into a tree that lives for thousands of years—reaching for heaven and giving shade to the earth.

3

WHICH CHILD IS GIFTED?

THE MOST important step in helping the gifted child is the first one—discovering and identifying his gifts. Once this has been accomplished, he can never again be treated just as any other child. He is different. Because he is different, he has some special needs.

The sooner this identification is made, the better. You cannot give the child the help he needs at home, at school, or in his religious setting until you know the extent and direction of his gifts. This knowledge will serve to guide your help, its kind and amount. Some children are stunted by too little encouragement, while others are stifled by too much. It is an established fact that some gifted children go through life unrecognized and un-challenged, while others become frustrated misfits because they were presumed to have gifts they did not possess. For these reasons it is vitally important that a child's gifts be identified as early, as thoroughly, and as carefully as possible.

Public schools are doing more and more to discover the differences and the gifts of their children. Batteries of highly sophisticated tests turn their searching lights on every child, seeking out his individual differences and gifts and measuring them. But in the home and especially in the church and syna-gogue the differences that make a child an individual are not generally sought out and measured. This unfortunate situation obtains not only because the testing and measuring procedures used in public schools would be impractical, but also because up to now little need has been felt to do so.

In my extensive investigation of the church and its gifted children, I have not yet discovered one church or church school that makes what can be considered valid evaluation of individual differences in its children. In spite of the fact that the religious and educational needs of these children are different, the gifted and creative children go undiscovered, unidentified and neglected.

1467687

Problems of Identification

Before we discuss some practical methods of identifying gifted children in the religious setting, it would be well to consider some difficulties. The talented and gifted child is not always easy to recognize. Even experts do not always agree on what to look for. There are many reasons for this. Several of the most common are these:

1. The gifted child usually looks and acts like any other child, often even when he is very highly gifted—unless one knows how to distinguish the telltale signs of behavior that are characteristic of talent and high ability.

2. The gifted child, particularly if he is creative and individualistic, may be mistakenly considered a stubborn and rebellious troublemaker or a misfit.

3. There are many misleading and fallacious—though popular and widely accepted—conceptions of gifted children which may interfere with a valid identification.

4. Because of social stigma and the ridicule of their peers, gifted children sometimes do an extremely effective job of hiding their talents.

5. Physical disability or emotional problems sometimes tend to obscure talent. This is especially true if a minimal brain injury is involved in some way. More rarely a type of brain injury in average or subaverage intelligence may disguise itself by what seems to be an unusual talent. For instance, brain damage may masquerade as an extraordinary ability to memorize numbers.

6. In the home or religious group accurate and formal testing and measurement of a child's intelligence would be

quite difficult, even if desirable. Reliable tests are difficult to administer, and more difficult to interpret. Few teachers of religion and still fewer parents have the training needed for this purpose. Moreover, it is the general consensus of opinion that such information is best withheld from parents on the assumption that it might be misused or incite harmful attitudes. In the religious setting there might be the same difficulties, plus a good possibility that it might not be kept as confidential as it ought to be. This is not to say that some general information—or even classification such as average, bright, gifted, or highly gifted—would not be desirable and useful. Such broad identification is necessary if children are to be treated as individuals with individual needs; moreover, it is possible.

In any attempt to discover and evaluate the gifts of a child, every means available must be used. When making identifications by the observable characteristics of the child (and this is the method most strongly relied on in the home and religious setting), one should carefully observe these principles: Possession of several of the characteristics usually associated with gifted children does not necessarily show that a child is gifted. Nor does every really gifted child have every trait listed. There is no definite pattern. Sometimes the marks of giftedness are evenly and well developed, while in other cases certain features stand out strongly. Patterns can be strangely intermixed. Remember, each child is an individual, like no other child. In every case good common sense and caution are essential.

General Characteristics

Although there are no two gifted children alike, they do tend to have certain characteristics in common which set them off as a group different from other children. In the hope that it will be used wisely and carefully, here is a list of characteristics generally accepted as indicative of giftedness. Despite its length and the attempt to make it complete, the best it can do is indicate that a child *might be* gifted.

Contrary to the popular picture of the gifted child—which is more a caricature than a likeness—the gifted child is not skinny and puny, stoop-shouldered or flat chested, with an oversized head wearing thick glasses. (The glasses may be worn. Myopia, or nearsightedness, seems to have an above-average incidence among gifted children.) As a group gifted children have been shown by many studies to develop both physically and mentally ahead of other children. They tend to grow taller and heavier, with better physical coordination. The brains and good looks of gifted children would seem to disprove the "beautiful but dumb" adage. Most gifted children walk, talk, read, do number work, take to hobbies, and develop an interest in religion earlier than average children. Ordinarily, children who have higher intelligence also have better health, and make more adequate emotional adjustments.

The gifted child often seems to be old for his age. He is likely to make friends with older children or with adults. He seems to have a more than usual amount of poise, common sense, and sense of responsibility. Often he, and more often she, has an uncanny knack of putting words together in a way usually thought to be characteristic of much older children. He uses more words and bigger words. These abilities may be the first traits that suggest the label of giftedness.

Sometimes unnoticed, but usually present in giftedness, are highly developed moral and spiritual qualities that are concerned with ethical concepts, spiritual insights, moral understandings, and sensitivity to social relationships. A greater desire to please often conflicts with a strong pull to be a creative nonconformist. But the gifted child usually has an unusual ability to translate moral and spiritual understandings into conduct. This may tend to make him intolerant of unacceptable conduct, and will of a certainty make him extremely sensitive to inconsistencies in others. When the gifted child is adequately guided and challenged, he often becomes an outstanding religious thinker and leader.

Leta Hollingworth insisted that the gifted child's interest in things religious coincided with his mental age rather than his physical age. This means that when a gifted child reaches the mental age of about twelve, he is ready for admittance to full religious participation. Delay in learning religious beliefs and creeds and in active membership in religious fellowship will be dangerously frustrating.

One of the most widely known characteristics of the gifted child is his ability to learn more, more easily and quickly, than the average. He needs less explanation and repetition in order to learn. Drill and "busy work" are particularly irritating and frustrating, and textbooks crammed with insignificant details or meaningless continuity create resentment. Here is a typical reaction to a social studies text in junior high that used a traveling family for continuity and often spent several paragraphs describing getting on and off ships and airplanes: "Phooey on that junk! Let's get on with the real thing. That's just kid stuff. I don't see why they have to waste my time with it."

This precocity in learning shows itself early in ability to form sentences, using a large vocabulary, memorizing long nursery rhymes, often reading (without help) before going to school, and possessing an unusually large fund of knowledge about many things without more than average exposure to them. This knowledge may concern itself with unusual things such as extrasensory perception, rat experiments in learning, archeology, or craters on the moon, so that one may be inclined to wonder, "Where did he learn that?"

The gifted child shows a high degree of mental alertness, a sensitivity to external stimuli above the average. He is quick to notice anything that attracts his attention, and few things do not. He sees details the average child misses. He is especially sensitive to inconsistencies in the behavior of adults, as well as to many inconsistencies in his environment and life in general. The incongruencies and conflicts in religious beliefs and dogmas disturb him no end, and the typical reaction is to reject everyone and everything associated with them.

Curiosity, insatiable curiosity, characterizes the gifted child. He is interested in everything. He takes watches apart and cuts open animals just to see "what's inside." He asks questions not to get attention or to be sociable, but because he really wants to know. And it is not enough to answer his "whats," for he will have even more "whys." The information obtained becomes a part of his thinking and is rapidly incorporated and used at the first opportunity. Information or knowledge that conflicts with previous knowledge is accepted tentatively, at least, and is held as true until it is proven false to his own satisfaction. This tendency should be well understood by those who guide gifted children, and especially by those who teach religion to these children.

The gifted often have an abundance of mental energy that is used to tackle an amazing range of interests without seeming to tire. This unusual energy may account, in a large part, for the unpleasant designation of "grinds" when those with less energy think of gifted children. But they do have the ability to "pour" it on when they become interested in an engrossing self-initiated problem.

An outgrowth of this abundance of mental energy is persistence and an attention span that spurns ordinary children's distractions. It includes the ability to concentrate even to the exclusion of hunger pangs when tackling some interesting project. They do not flit from one interest to another, even though they may have, and usually do have, many interests. Gifted youngsters of only two or three may play for hours with the simplest toys. A boy I knew, when only two, would sit for several hours with a toy auto, which could be taken apart with a screwdriver. Sometimes this persistent concentration on an absorbing interest may cause the gifted child to neglect other things that ought to get some of his attention—like school work, or studies that have less interest value. In some cases this complete absorption and involvement in a matter that has captured his imagination excludes all other pursuits to a degree that appears unbalanced. The dedication to the interest area may be intense and the work brilliant, but no amount of persuasion will cause him to devote effort to any other matter. Obviously, this tendency could have drastic consequences under present standards of a liberal education and cause no end of frustration in the usual religious education situation.

Most gifted children find little satisfaction in easy or superficial tasks, but prefer and, if left on their own, will choose difficult problems which they are usually able to solve. They seem to enjoy new and unfamiliar situations that require intense mental effort. This includes academic studies as well as puzzles, games, and stories of mystery. Abstract ideas are of more interest to gifted children than to average children.

This intense interest in what might be called deep thinking probably is associated with their ability to reason and generalize, and to perceive subtle relationships. They seem to have a superior sense of what is relevant, and can discriminate between important and unimportant details. Those who are looking for signs of giftedness should watch carefully for the words *like* and *as,* since the ability to generalize results in the use of many similes and metaphors as they see similarities and make comparisons. This characteristic makes illogical spelling and strange verb tenses particularly frustrating. At the time it gives gifted children superior insight into difficult problems, and helps them to find a sound solution quickly. This swift insight often gives them sympathetic understanding of others and why they act or feel as they do. The bright child often perceives why another child is sad or unhappy, angry or fearful, and makes allowances for these moods. He incessantly asks others and himself "Why?" and diligently tries to find answers.

Gifted children usually come equipped with a highly developed "self-starter," which is an unusual ability to see what needs to be done. If they do not have the knowledge needed for action, or for solutions of the problem, they set about acquiring that knowledge. And more, they usually finish what they start. This self-reliance and confidence is neither quickly baffled nor easily discouraged if they are allowed to carry on their investigations. However, they can be disastrously frustrated by interference and disapproval from those they love and respect.

Memory seems to pose a paradox. Many very bright children profess to have no memory powers, but memory usually is directly proportional to intellectual capacity. The gifted seem to have little difficulty memorizing material they are going to use. A possible solution may lie in the fact that most gifted children detest rote learning or memory work; detail without apparent significance is hated "busy work." A gifted physics student expressed his feelings: "Why should I bother to memorize all those formulae when I can find them in any text or handbook?" Gifted children are often atrocious spellers, and are slow to memorize the multiplication tables. A better clue to their high memory potential lies in a large vocabulary, wide fund of general knowledge, and ability to recall facts learned weeks or months previously.

Achievement in school, as measured by standardized tests, is many times two to four years beyond their grade placement. This is true especially in language arts (not spelling!), arithmetic reasoning (not facts!), science, and the social studies. They are often weak in handwriting, which may be due to the desire to write as fast as they think or to the belief that writing is a bothersome yet necessary chore that slows them down. Some authorities explain the poor handwriting on the basis of poor manual coordination, but this seems unlikely in view of the fact that gifted children usually have superior muscular coordination. It would seem their general attitude toward troublesome details would have more bearing here. However, they normally like school and show a desire to learn without prodding, easily mastering the subject. But their achievement may be only sufficient to get by, because they may be bored sick with the slow pace or uninspired methods of teaching. In some cases, they deliberately cut back their achievement in order to escape the designation of "brain" or "grind." Under ideal and challenging situations, however, they like school and show preference for the more difficult subjects.

An interesting peculiarity of exceptionally able children is their interest in time. Clocks and calendars, the concept of yesterday and tomorrow, and history and the hereafter get their attention at an early age. They often show a great deal of foresight and are able to postpone satisfaction for far greater periods than one would expect. The origin of the universe and its end, its significance; the purpose, meaning, and destiny of life—these concerns are intense and appear early. The ability to profit from experience and to foresee what may happen in situations similar to previous experience seems exceptional.

Collecting things often of an unusual complicated nature is

characteristic of gifted boys and girls. Whether it is stamps, butterflies, chemicals, archaeological artifacts, or pictures of television stars, it is done with a high degree of orderliness and thoroughness. Their hobbies are numerous and precocious in comparison with other children of the same age, and they may have a dozen different projects going at once in orderly fashion.

Children with high intelligence usually have a highly developed sense of humor and a creative wit. Their brand of humor is mature and subtle, rather than broad and slapstick—although this does not rule out laughter at a well executed pratfall or pie in the face. Their tendency is toward abstract or ironical twists. Puns are favorites. They also can laugh at themselves and see the humor in predicaments. While their reading is often of a quite advanced and serious nature for their age, do not be disappointed if they take great delight in the popular comic books, or if they choose to watch Red Skelton or Bob Hope in preference to an informative documentary. This does not mean that they find everything funny as is sometimes the case with retarded children. Gifted children hve a high discriminatory ability, and it includes what they find amusing. Their ability to create wit and humor is just as important as their ability to see the funny side of things.

An outstanding characteristic of intellectually gifted children is originality. This creative ability may show itself in original ways of using words, playing games, eating, washing dishes, or wearing clothes. Or it may be seen in what some call more practical matters such as writing, invention, and better ways of doing old things. Whatever direction it takes, it demonstrates the unusual and important ability to see new relationships and get new ideas. It may or may not include the ability to make practical applications.

Creativity often makes high intellectual ability a troublesome gift. It usually leads to nonconformity. Some educators have observed that children are more creative than adults. Their minds are open and unshackled. The restricting chains of conformity have not yet been wound around the soaring inventive intellect. Their expression is seldom orthodox, and new approaches or solutions are not always acceptable or even right.

If sufficient pressure is exerted and the child is at all pliable, individuality may be smothered. If a creative child persists in his nonconforming thinking and originality, he becomes a misfit who appears to be, or is, rebellious. In school, he may be an underachiever. In his religious group he is a "bad" boy.

Creativity is little understood, probably because it has, until recently, received little attention. In several recent studies of highly creative people, it was found that most of them made rather poor grades in school. One wonders why this is true. A higher percentage of girls are better students, at least through high school, than boys. Are girls less creative, or do they tend toward more conformity?

These questions are raised to point out that creativity, generally characteristic of gifted children, is a very complex and confusing gift. It follows no uniform pattern. Great care must be used in its detection and evaluation, and more in its nurture and encouragement. (Creativity will be considered more in Chapter 6.) The original and creative children will become the true leaders of religious life and, indeed, of society.

Socially, gifted children find themselves in a dilemma. They have a tremendous desire to be loved and accepted by their peers and by adults, but at the same time they are different and act in nonconforming ways. More than the average child they want to be of real service to society, but they can be snobbish and critical, even intolerant of others with less talent. Nevertheless, they excel in such traits as cheerfulness, leadership, thoughtfulness, prudence, sympathy, tenderness, generosity, truthfulness, freedom from vanity, and conscientiousness. But they may not be very humble. They are usually quite eager to help others at home, school, or in the religious setting. Not infrequently they can be spotted by their ready responses when you ask for help, and then they efficiently proceed to carry the task to completion.

Last on the list, but by no means the least, is the gifted child's tendency to self-criticism and moral anxiety. Insight, critical judgment, knowledge, and an unusual ability to make evaluations—accompanying manifestations of this tendency—have their dangers as well as good points. Not only is he likely to be overly conscientious; but because his sense of moral values develops earlier than in most children, the home, school, church or synagogue may not be ready to help him understand his problems in this area. He may flounder, developing all sorts of guilt feelings long before parents or teachers come to his rescue. He may be disturbed far more than they realize by the moral aspects of unfair treatment of others. It has been observed that many gifted children weep when they read *Uncle Tom's Cabin,* or of the bombing of Hiroshima, or see pictures of Vietnamese war horror. They seem to accept personal responsibility and even guilt for group actions. They set high standards for themselves, their family, and their religious group. Seldom are they profane or lewd. These moral qualities probably develop because they perceive what is needed or expected, and foresee possible consequences.

Are gifts and talents related? This is an area of dispute. Some authorities hold that talents are special abilities, while others maintain that talents are specific functions of high general intelligence. The latter believe that children with specific abilities must first have superior mental ability which takes off in a particular direction because of motivational factors such as emotional values and interest, experience, encouragement, and opportunity. Furthermore, this school of thought continues, if an individual has one talent he probably has many special abilities which could be developed. But most people think of talents as specialized and isolated abilities which may or may not depend upon high general intelligence. Obviously we stand to learn much more about talents and giftedness. However, at the present time, the evidence seems to indicate that unusual intelligence is basic to many, if not all, talents.

Special Manifestations

Giftedness in the arts is probably the most difficult type of talent to identify accurately. Intelligence tests now in use do not measure or discover creativity, and the newer tests for creativity or originality are not in general use. Aptitude and interest tests, although valuable in some areas, do not adequately measure giftedness in art, music, drama, or the dance. Even the Seashore music test, long considered valid, is only an indicator at best. Still we must depend for the most part on careful observation, looking for interest and achievement in any art that is far above that what is expected of an average child. The opinion of experts in any field of art will also be of value. A number of specialized schools depend on this method of evaluation for admission.

In music look for the child's reaction to music he hears. Note his enjoyment and response to it with regard to qualities in pitch and tone, rhythm and tempo. Does he show ability to memorize tunes or passages, and initiative in learning musical numbers or playing some instrument?

Talent in art can best be observed by the kind and quality of pictures or drawings the child makes or the models he carves out.

In the dance watch for intense interest, physical grace and coordination or movement, and a great sense of rhythm. If these are present, then you might try a few lessons by a competent instructor, choosing the best to be found.

Creative writing shows itself most obviously by the ability to put words together in interesting and meaningful ways, on paper. Not all glib and interesting talkers can put their thoughts down in logical order. Many excellent writers are poor speakers. Originality and imagination are very essential ingredients, as are interest and a desire to write.

Giftedness in things mechanical is not necessarily indicated by the ability to keep a "heap" or "rod" (car, that is) running. Americans generally show considerable ability to understand mechanical gadgets of all sorts, but unusual ingenuity and inventiveness in solving mechanical problems may indicate talent in this area. Mechanical ability often is associated with high skill in mathematics and a high level of general intelligence. Aptitude tests may be of some value here, but they reveal deficiencies in mechanical ability far better than they indicate giftedness.

An unusual but important kind of giftedness, which could be invaluable in religious vocations or social service, is what may be called social talent—the ability to sense the feelings and social attitudes of others, and the ability to get along with people, even to manipulate them. While this gift can often be observed quite early in life, more than many other talents it can be adversely affected and even obscured by environmental influences. Personal relationships in the home are particularly instrumental in this regard. This gift shows itself by intense interest in others, chiefly by a desire to be helpful and of service. Those so gifted are skilled in games and often suggest things to do in a group. They treat other children well, and often stand up for the rights of the underdog. Because they are leaders, they are often the eager volunteers who as adults carry most of the load of community service, are the busy people in church or synagogue. They become ministers, rabbis, and political leaders.

This does not, by any means, exhaust the list of special manifestations of giftedness. You may want to add physical skill and sports, dramatic ability, homemaking, and manual dexterity. Those interested in religion will include spiritual insights and ethical understandings, as well as high moral values with conduct to match.

How to Identify Giftedness

Earlier in this chapter caution was urged in making a valid identification of the gifts of a child. More must be said. Never compare one child with another—no two children are alike in looks or giftedness. Any child, gifted or not, is different from any other child. One of the most difficult things to do in this age of togetherness and conformity is to accept that difference, and, more, to make the most of it.

Consider carefully all the characteristics and aptitudes of a child before concluding that he is or is not gifted. Not every child who talks glibly, or memorizes easily, or likes to draw or plays the piano, or takes clocks apart possesses talents in these areas. On the other hand, some very docile and quiet children give only rare and occasional glimpses of their unusual ability. Consider the whole child, with his purposes, interests, and achievements. Remember that a child for various reasons may not have developed the characteristics generally possessed by most gifted children, and that the configuration may be unusual.

However, the error in identification is more apt to be in underestimating rather than overestimating a child's ability. This is true even when various tests are used and accepted as good indicators of ability. There is little chance that a child will appear brighter or test higher than his real ability, but there are many forces at work to obscure ability. In identification by testing such factors as illness, fatigue, emotional stress, and lack of interest or motivation will hinder the best response. Note also that most group IQ tests are not designed to measure high ability. In a study of highly gifted children, I would have failed to discover 82 per cent had group IQ test results only been used.

When identification is made by observation alone, talent will most often be obscured by the fact that gifted children for the most part look and act as do most average children to the casual observer. The uninformed often mistake a glib tongue, nice manners, good behavior, strong interest, or bright eyes as indicators of giftedness. Of course the bright child may have bright eyes and a glib tongue, but more evidence than this is needed to make an accurate appraisal of ability.

Since giftedness usually appears early in life, identification will start in the home. To the knowing observer, many of the characteristics of ability can be seen before the child enters school. More than actual performance, the careful observer looks for appropriateness of response and what sets it off. Gifted children respond to smaller clues and less stimulus than do average children.

After a child has entered school, his interest and grades may or may not give an indication of giftedness. Some gifted children do just enough to get by, but they rarely fail. Some average children are hard workers and overachievers. Conferences with a child's teacher, who no doubt has some test results at hand, will be a helping factor, Actual scores often will be withheld, but some valid indication usually will be offered. Watching a child at play with other children will give other clues. Sometimes other adults, friends, relatives, a physician, or a minister may observe characteristics a parent has missed, or confirm what he has found.

Reading habits, hobbies, interests, general information, vocabulary—all must be considered. It is of the utmost importance to rely on no single indicator for valid appraisal of a child's gifts. *Use every means available.*

If, then, there is still considerable doubt, consult an expert, such as the school's psychological services or those of a nearby college or university. Please note the term *psychologist*. The psychiatrist is a medical doctor who specializes in mental diseases and emotional disturbances. The psychologist, especially the educational psychologist, is a specialist in the science of learning and its problems, and is familiar with testing procedures that evaluate intelligence, achievement, and aptitudes.

Identification in the Religious Setting

The identification of gifted children in church and synagogue poses severe problems. For one thing, the religious educator in these organizations sees his pupil rarely more than once a week, sometimes only an hour, and the director of religious education, pastor, or rabbi probably sees the child even less. Formal testing of intelligence or aptitude is out of the question for the obvious reason of lack of time, and the less obvious but more important factor of lack of training and skill in administering and evaluating such tests. Furthermore, if such tests were possible, it might be extremely difficult to keep the test results confidential.

But the matter of identification in the religious group is not hopeless even if it may seem difficult. Any such institution, large or small, that wants to identify gifted children can follow these suggestions:

1. Consult the parents of the pupil and discuss his interests and abilities with them. This will take a lot of time, but you will never be able to treat that child as before, even if he is not gifted. And if he is, you may better be able to help him develop a secure religious faith.

2. The pupil's school teacher or principal, if properly approached, many times will be able to help in evaluation of his ability. The pastor, rabbi, or director of religious education may be able to obtain such information for most of the children in his group. In some school systems the officials are not permitted to give out test results; however, they may be able to give an indication of general ability. This information may be better than a test score which may need special knowledge to interpret. In some instances, a clue to ability may be found in the school's group placement of the pupil. However, care should be used to determine the basis for grouping. If grouping is strict and made on the basis of ability, it can be helpful; if it is made on the basis of achievement, or is "modified," it will be of little value.

3. Even though a child is in the religious education group only a short time, if his teacher knows what to look for, he can learn a great deal—from his interests, the questions he asks, his relationships with the other children, his willingness to volunteer, and the like. Thorough familiarity with the general characteristics of gifted children will be valuable.

4. The observations of other religious leaders will be of some value. The pastor or rabbi should be of most assistance in some evaluation of the child's talents. This is particularly true if he, too, is familiar with the general characteristics of gifted children and their psychology. He probably has been in the child's home a number of times and knows the parents and their background, as well as that of the child.

5. There are several formal tests now available which can be adapted for use in the religious school for identification purposes. However, they should be used with care and in connection with the above suggestions. Keep the scores confidential, and do not jump to conclusions solely on this one of many indicators of giftedness. A list of short easy-to-use tests is included at the end of the annotated bibliography of this book.

If you discover a gifted child in the religious group or at home, remember that he is still a child who is in most respects like any other child. How he should be treated, and how he can be helped will be discussed in the chapters that follow.

4

SOME RELIGIOUS PROBLEMS OF THE GIFTED CHILD

"Prevention is better than cure" has been stated so often that it has become a cliché. But the fact still remains. In this chapter we will consider some of the problems of the gifted child in the hope that many of them can be prevented, and we entertain the hope that some of them can be cured as well. These problems are presented with no implication of criticism or blame, but with the conviction that difficulties that are identified and understood are far easier to work with, perhaps solve, than are those which go undefined.

Many of the problems faced by the gifted child in the religious education environment are similar to, if not the same, as those experienced in the secular education environment. Of course there are other problems which are peculiar to the religious setting.

But whatever the problem and wherever it is found, most often it is due to ignorance and lack of understanding of the gifted child's special needs and of the problems that grow out of his differences. In terms of time, our understanding of the peculiarities of giftedness and the difficulties encountered by the superior child is as only yesterday. There is also a time lag between the latest educational developments and practices in secular education and the adoption of the best of these in religious education. Not all public schools by any means have put into practice all we know about the gifted. It cannot be expected that the religious institution will have been able to do better. It is to these facts that we address ourselves as we take a hard look at some problems of the gifted child.

The religious problems of the gifted child grow directly out of the conflict between certain innate and generally accepted characteristics of the gifted child and certain common practices and attitudes that are found in the usual religious education situation in the religious institution or at home. This inherent incompatibility bores and baffles most gifted children. Yet it has developed so slowly and insidiously that few parents or teachers of religion are aware that the gifted child *has* any problems with religion. Parents have long been aware of the fact that in spite of the best religious training they could give their children, some of them turned against their religion. And leaders in the church school have known for decades that many children drop out and fall along the wayside, and that others become mischievous troublemakers. What they are not aware of is this fact: among the dropouts and troublemakers are most of the gifted children.

The religious home and the religious institution begin their relationship with gifted children with a unique advantage—an earlier and greater interest in matters pertaining to religion. It is a misfortune beyond our comprehension that a number of insidious and destructive conflicts often cancel out this underestimated advantage and even turn gifted children against religion. Understanding should help us to regain this advantage and guide us to ways of leading gifted children to a secure and reasonable faith.

The gifted child can no more help the way he reacts intellectually to new or conflicting ideas than he can help that he is gifted in the first place. It does no good to say that he should accept what is taught because the Bible or religious authority says thus and so, or that he is a "bad" boy who lacks "faith." This approach will serve only to create more conflicts. He must be understood in order to understand.

Common Areas of Conflict

The innate characteristics generally found in gifted children which most often clash with certain traditional religous concepts and practices can be grouped into six major categories or syndromes. They will vary, of course, from child to child and from religious setting to religious setting in degree and configuration, but some conflicts will usually be found in each of these areas:

1. *First and foremost the gifted child is different.* True, he usually looks just like other less talented children and he may act like them in many ways. But he thinks differently, has more imagination, creativity and originality, and he has more initiative and desire to do things on his own. He has a wider curiosity, and he thinks reflectively. All of this is reinforced by the fact that he is more receptive to new ideas which he holds as true until he proves them false to his own satisfaction. Therefore, new ideas that come to him as a result of reading or his own imagination and originality are accepted, tentatively at least.

   The fact that gifted children are self-reliant and resourceful—rather than dependent, submissive, and humble—aggravates many of the conflicts they have. These latter traits, so many times regarded as essential attitudes in one's relationship to God and religion, are recessive and uncommon in the gifted. It is difficult for adults, who do not understand that these personality traits are characteristic, to realize that these children are not being mean or rebellious. It just happens that this firm autonomy is part of their being gifted. Among gifted children passive submission is a rare quality; instead, we find an active outgoing and self-reliant creativity.

   However, rebellion should not be ruled out as a possible, and desirable, reaction to religious frustration. Rebellion should be recognized as a symptom rather than a malady. It indicates that there is a problem that needs understanding and treatment. It should be recognized as tension which normally will cause a change in adaptive behavior for the better, if handled properly. The wise parent or teacher of religion will accept this attitude or reaction and seek to understand the child's feelings, with an attempt to modify the causes.

This same configuration of characteristics of gifted children often creates another problem. It is a well-known fact among educators that many teachers tend to equate giftedness with "good" behavior, conformity, and submissiveness, and to categorize troublemakers and non-conformists as somewhat less gifted. My studies indicate that this is also true in the religious education setting, as is revealed by many statements such as this: "We do not lose the really gifted children; we lose mostly the disinterested (nonconforming) troublemakers."

Fortunately there is an increasing tendency in recent years among some religious groups to emphasize the development of independent thinking and autonomy with regard to religious convictions and viewpoints. Yet on the other hand, the most common viewpoint of religion still demands literal acceptance of quite inflexible creeds and dogmas, as well as conformity to rather well defined behavior patterns. While the more liberal faiths tolerate divergencies more than do the conservative ones, the general trend in many religious groups is to resist the independent and nonconforming thinker with rather strict sanctions. This is also true in the public school. The autonomous creative thinker becomes an oddball who is hard to understand, or he is considered a misfit and outcast. The penetrating and disturbing questions he asks are either unanswered, or they are parried with flat dogmas and vague generalities. They may even be taken as an indication of malicious unbelief. Only rarely are they understood for what they are—the sincere quest of a searching mind for truth.

On top of all this most children, and especially gifted children, are taught in schools to learn by examining, questioning, and thinking reflectively. Modern education places a great deal of emphasis upon the philosophy that we know only that which we can test or experience with our senses. In school, from books, and on television children discover facts that appear to be inconsistent with religion as it is often taught. For most gifted children the quest for a reasonable faith in religious beliefs has become increasingly difficult in this day of scientific method. In school reflective thinking is "premiumized," while in too many religious settings it is penalized.

Happily more and more religious groups are changing their approach to creative materials in the religious education experience. A trend is developing toward truly meaningful and creative learning activities. But when the "creative" media used in religious education programs consists of merely busy work prepared by a religious publishing house or the teacher, and the pupil "expresses himself" mainly by following directions to complete a project already half done, initiative and originality are penalized early.

In the religious education situation we find the gifted child with an inherent urge to use all of his God-given talent of creativity, logical thinking, and curiosity to find reasonable answers to all of his questions. But far too often he is asked to conform to the creedal standards of his group and to accept on faith without question all the creeds and beliefs of his religion.

Thus, this whole complex of his innate characteristics, attitudes, and ways of thinking are in violent conflict with the customary approach to religion. Obviously, then, when the gifted child's new ideas or ways of thinking or questions differ from the customary views and beliefs of the religion he is being taught, serious questions fill his mind. He finds it extremely difficult to conform, but many times he does want to. Gifted children, as do other children, want approval and may go to great lengths to secure it.

If this approach to religion is persisted in with the gifted child, one or more of several deplorable consequences are almost certain to follow. He may reject the religious institution along with its creeds and doctrines altogether. He may choose an extremely liberal form of religion, a common choice. In a number of instances the gifted child has been known to pretend to conform to what he feels his elders and peers want. Tremendously persistent and destructive guilt feelings may grip him if he feels that he is unable to be a "good believer." Agnosticism and cynicism become his dominant philosophy. He may try to close his mind to truth, accepting only that which conforms to previously held beliefs and dogmas, which will produce no end of other conflicts and anxieties. He may withdraw from social contact with adults and peers because he feels rejected as one who cannot conform. Except for the turning to a liberal faith (and this is a matter of conviction), these are deviant and destructive responses. But they are all too often the responses conciously or unconsciously elicited by prevalent religious instruction.

2. *The gifted child learns easier with less repetition and drill.* He memorizes quicker and remembers longer, has longer attention span, and prefers to learn on his own.

Yet in the average religious education situation, particularly in the church school, no consideration is made as to whether the child has studied or has been taught religion before or not. He may be well versed in his faith or he may know nothing at all, but he is usually lumped together with all children his age or grade in school. I have been unable to find any religious education program where objective considerations of any kind were used to determine development and individual differences in children, although this concept has been the most revolutionary idea to hit education in the last century. No objective measurements of any kind are used to discover how quickly a child, gifted or not, can learn, or how much he has learned.

As a result many children will be bored and frustrated by repetition of what they already know, while others will be baffled because they have little or no background from which to learn. No knowledgeable secular educator would tolerate this situation for long.

Compounding these difficulties for the gifted child is the fact that most of the teaching of religion, whether in the home or the religious institution consists of pouring out information like water over little jugs in the tranquilizing hope that some will fall in. Gifted children resent such instruction. They find the ordinary kind of memorizing dull, and drill irritating. Instead, they like to attempt difficult tasks for which they can use their self-starting ability, examine evidence, and form their own conclusions. True, they need guidance, but not predigested information, and the difference is fundamental. This is a matter of methods of teaching more than it is one of subject matter or content.

These are some of the severest criticisms that can be leveled at the average religious institution. The conditions which prompt them must adversely affect average children as well as the bright and gifted.

3. *Highly intelligent children are alarmingly observant and keenly sensitive to inconsistencies.* They notice, in particular, illogical and contradictory relationships in concepts and ideas, and the contradictions between ideals and practice. Especially disturbing are the troublesome inconsistencies sometimes found in the lives of people in positions of authority. In all cases, gifted children tend toward what is called "negative suggestibility," the predominant tendency to reject everyone and everything associated with incongruent thinking and living.

All of life is filled with troublesome contradictions and confusing inconsistencies, but nowhere are they more obvious and perplexing than in religion, which usually sets a high standard of moral and ethical living and which traditionally purports to have the "truth." The more rigid the moral code and the more dogmatic the "truth," the more unresolvable and unacceptable do the inconsistencies become. In gifted children the result is often rebellion against authority as well as rejection of religion. The wound in mind and soul may heal, but more often than not a disabling scar remains for life.

4. *There is a greater and earlier degree of religious development in gifted children.* What should be a powerful advan-

tage can be a harassing problem. Many religious groups have long believed and practiced the concept that religious accountability begins about the age of twelve. When children reach this age, they are taught the beliefs of the particular group and accepted into membership in the congregation. Leta Hollingworth and others insist that children begin to ask searching questions about the universe, the purpose of life, the destiny of men, the reason for creation, and God's place in it all—questions for which religion seeks to provide the answers at least in some measure—when they reach the *mental age* of about twelve. Therefore, the higher the intelligence the earlier the pressing need for religious instruction occurs. This can occur as early as seven or eight years of age.

Gifted children need help to find adequate answers to their religious questions far earlier than is commonly supposed. True, some religion is taught to most children before they reach twelve, but it consists mostly of simple stories and superficial instruction in beliefs and doctrine. The thinking child has a surprising fund of disturbing questions that should be considered long before they usually are. Delay frustrates and injures him.

5. *Gifted children show a marked tendency to self-criticism and moral anxiety.* No doubt there is some relationship between this and the item above, but I feel that it needs special consideration as a potential troublemaker in religion.

Conscientiousness, knowledge, and imagination are valuable characteristics of giftedness, but they can also give rise to abnormal feelings of guilt, unworthiness, and a sense of insecurity. These feelings are allowed to grow out of neglect by parents and teachers who do not anticipate them as early as they appear. Who would think that children of three or four are *really* concerned about death and its consequences as expressed by one frightened child: "My puppy's mommy went to heaven and left him alone. What if my mommy goes to heaven?"

Children with superior intelligence are troubled by the

suffering of others. One such youngster when told of the bombing of Hiroshima was found crying long after he was put to bed. After considerable persuasion to tell why, he said, "I can't help thinking about all those boys and girls that got burned up."

Because of this sensitivity and a strong sense of responsibility coupled with strict self-evaluation, they often experience guilt long before most adults realize the possibility. They set high standards for their friends, their family, their community, and themselves. These standards are often not realistic and consequently are not reached. Again, feelings of failure and guilt arise.

Not only do gifted children feel indignant at injustice, and suffer vicariously when others suffer, but they sometimes will actively seek to set matters right, butt into matters not their concern, and become obnoxiously bossy. These tendencies have an excellent chance to persist into adulthood.

The problem lies not in the innate tendency of gifted children to feel or act as they do in moral matters; the problem lies in the failure of parents and religious leaders to recognize these characteristics early enough to guide the children into proper and healthy attitudes.

6. *Characteristic of most gifted children is their search for a purpose.* They seek a reason for being; they exert a drive to accomplish something of real worth. In religious matters this quest unfortunately turns out to be a baffling and frustrating desire in most cases. Confused by unacceptable answers to questions about God, bored by the customary methods of teaching religion, disgusted by unresolved conflicts with inconsistencies, filled with guilt because of injustice and unmerited suffering, and alienated by lack of understanding by those they respect and love, gifted children hardly are led by the usual approach to religion to find an eternal purpose for living or a spiritual reason for being.

A few become fanatical reformers, a few more are fortunate enough to be guided into a constructive and rea-

sonable faith, some live out a life of meaningless unful-
filled existence, but most of them reject religion and project their great talent and drive into endeavors unrelated
to and unguided by religion.

Problems Inherent in Most Religious
Education Programs

Accentuating and compounding the above problems of the
gifted child are a number of weaknesses and attitudes inherent
in the philosophy and program of the groups and institutions
dedicated to religious education:

1. Historically religious institutions resist change and reform. New methods of teaching, modern attitudes toward
   children, revealing insights and conceptions of "truth"
   if they differ from the old—all are too often vigorously
   opposed by those who consider changes as heresy. For
   some reason what is "old" is too often valued far more
   than what is "new" in religion. (This is one fundamental
   reason why there are so many denominations. An eminent
   theologian once said, "You cannot reform a church; you
   can only start a new one.")
2. The church teaches the child only about an hour a week,
   often less. Attendance is voluntary, and often irregular.
   Obviously the home is in a far better position in this
   respect, but unfortunately most homes have remanded
   their responsibility in religion to the religious institution.
3. While most teachers of religion are sincere and dedicated
   to their task, many of them are unskilled, untrained, and
   often uninteresting. Some churches require some training
   for their teachers, but most church school directors are
   happy to use whoever is willing to take a class. At the top
   of the list of recommendations of gifted students with
   good religious background is "better teachers."
4. Most religious education materials and "creative" work
   is designed for the average child, if not low average. It

would take the best efforts of a highly skilled teacher to
interest a gifted child in them.

5. The popularly held idea that the gifted child "can take
care of himself" and that "genius will out" is reinforced
by the Scripture-based belief that the "one-talent" individual is more likely to bury his gifts than the "ten-talent"
person, with the result that more attention and encouragement are given to the less able child. It is often considered
neither ethical nor democratic to do otherwise.

All of the foregoing problems of gifted children with religion
are the more deeply entrenched in lethargy and resignation by a
popular and strongly held tranquilizing attitude. Dr. Ronald
Doll of Columbia University, an educator and interested church
layman, writes:

Though the Sunday school seems to limp along, it often accomplishes wonders. Only an all-wise God could use untrained volunteers, meager physical facilities, and limited materials to change the
course of so many lives. Handicaps that would stagger the secular
educator are met by the unprepared but faithful teacher and superintendent, and the Lord gets for himself and us a victory.

After considerable study and investigation of the gifted child
and his religion, this writer is led to one conclusion above all
others: The gifted and creative child *must have special help* to
find for himself a vital and creative faith if he is to have any
faith at all.

Special Problems of the Gifted Adolescent

Any problem that gifted children have with religion is in-
tensified in adolescence. Their rapid physical growth, new feelings and emotions, the struggle for independence and recognition as an individual—all combine to complicate other problems. It is during this period that religious concepts and values
undergo the greatest change, and it is significant that also during this period the greatest loss of children from the church
takes place.

It should be noted that most adolescents, including the gifted, possess some kind of religious faith and that most of them attend church rather regularly. As a group they take religion seriously, possessing an intimate and inclusive set of beliefs.

Most of their concepts and attitudes toward life are based on this faith. Though problems with religion cause lifelong problems, we must face the sobering fact that most gifted adolescents become bored and baffled by religion by the time they reach their late teens, if not sooner.

If religious instruction has been mainly a set of generalized abstractions, or doctrines memorized the same as the names of the states, they have little upon which to build. If their parents have preached a gospel of love but have demonstrated no real affection toward them, no religious indoctrination can fill the void. Sharp discrepancies between professed standards and practiced attitudes create a sense of worthlessness in any child, but even more so in the gifted and sensitive adolescent. Most destructive are critical attitudes and practices. While careless criticism may harm the one who is attacked, it unfailingly destroys the innocent but interested bystander—in this case the gifted teen-ager.

A problem that has not received attention in proportion to the harm it causes is the attraction to religion of persons who have not been able to accept themselves or win the acceptance of others. Affiliation with a religious group rarely changes these persons, and they remain hostile, unbending, critical, and unloving. Their self-condemnation often is externalized and they have a tendency to be fanatics who are intolerant and unforgiving. While they are to be pitied, for no doubt the hurt they give springs from hurt received, it is not easy to estimate the untold harm these sometimes "pillars" of the church have caused by their ardent and faithful intolerance. It is reasonable to believe that many bitter adolescents who leave the church have been "set straight" by these anxious and unloving church members. The gifted child with his high sensitivity will be hurt the most.

The tendency toward self-evaluation and self-criticism characteristic of gifted children reaches its peak in adolescence. Such self-examination is a sign of healthy growth. Concepts of self, ideals, and religious beliefs which are usually taken for granted in childhood, having been received secondhand from adults close to them, must now be carefully reevaluated to become their own. The more sure the adolescent is of himself and his convictions, the less trouble he will have. If he has learned to have an open mind, he will have the courage to question his beliefs; what is doubt to others may become belief to him.

Trouble arises in these matters when the gifted adolescent has not been taught how to question, think reflectively, and form his own conclusions with an open mind. He may have been taught, as many have, that questioning is especially wrong in religion. Untold feelings of guilt are then almost inevitable, for he feels compelled to do that which he has been taught not to do.

Dogmas that were accepted blandly at ten or twelve are questioned. Claim made for religion such as peace and happiness may not be found in those who talk most about them. The conception of creation, the validity of miracles, and the meaning of prayer all may very well undergo a radical change during adolescence. Fortunate indeed is that gifted child who has parents and teachers who do not condemn but who understand.

Sometimes parents and church leaders may neither condemn nor understand, but resignedly accept the questioning and revision of religious beliefs as "just one of those things" that all adolescents must go through. They comfort themselves in the belief that it's just a stage of growth, that after a few years these children will return as adults to the faith of their childhood. My studies reveal that this is wishful thinking for the most part. Very few gifted adolescents who leave their religious group ever return to it. A few do for social or business reasons and many later seek a more liberal faith, but most are lost to a meaningful and vital religion of any kind. They did not receive the help they needed when they needed it most.

5

HELPING THE GIFTED CHILD
WITH RELIGION

THIS chapter is concerned with basic attitudes and general practices which will help the gifted child. Subsequent chapters will deal in greater detail with methods as they affect areas of development about which religious education programs and the home are, or ought to be, concerned.

Careful identification and informed understanding of the gifted child are indispensable to any other help you can give him and are singularly effective in themselves. These first steps are basic. Then what else can we do to help gifted children find a reasonable and secure faith?

My investigations have discovered a few talented and creative children who find what they need in religion. Almost invariably these children have been guided by unusually understanding and accepting parents who themselves have found a satisfying and secure faith or by an effectively discerning teacher or minister. More rarely they have belonged to a religious group that has developed a special program to help its gifted children. Let us consider several typically gifted children in these untypical situations.

How Three Churches Do It

Allen attends a rare and unusual church which is located in the suburb of a large city. For about seven years now he has been instructed by church school teachers who are carefully selected on the basis of their love for children and their own firm beliefs, which will withstand critical reexamination. These teachers receive training in the basic doctrines of the church, but special emphasis is placed upon methods of recognizing and identifying individual differences in children like Allen. They also receive some training in methods of teaching, with particular stress on leading their pupils to ask questions, discuss ideas, and think reflectively.

Ever since Allen has been in these classes, he has been encouraged to ask questions and to talk about anything that troubles him. He has been stimulated to read and to investigate on his own and to instigate projects related to religion. But above all, he has been led to form his own conclusions. There are no pat answers, stiff dogmas, or inflexible creeds to be learned or memorized. Any answer that meets his spiritual, emotional, and intellectual needs is the right answer. His religious teachers work in the conviction that their religion basically is a creative faith. It is flexible enough to meet the religious needs of people of every age and every culture. There has always been room for inspired and creative thinkers, such as Moses, Hosea, Paul, Thomas of Aquinas, Martin Luther, Karl Barth, Martin Buber, and Albert Schweitzer.

For children younger than Allen and too immature to discuss complex religious beliefs, the activities consist mostly of directed play, rhythm movements, music, and really creative art. The teacher usually reads or tells a story. At about five years they begin to ask questions and share their feelings and ideals. Simple forms of worship are begun at about the sixth year of age. Throughout respect for God, ethics, morality, and human relationships are stressed. Few doctrines and beliefs are considered until about the tenth year. Beliefs about God that foster fear or guilt are carefully avoided.

No attempt is made to provide special groups or classes for the gifted, although children may be shifted to another class if it is felt that they may get along better with the teacher or other children. Each teacher uses whatever materials and methods he feels are necessary to meet the individual needs of each child.

It seems that this program provides a natural environment for stimulating and teaching its bright and gifted children.

Considerable attention is given to Allen's parents and the parents of all the children in the church school. Special classes are provided for them. Reading is encouraged, especially authoritative books on child care and development, psychology, social adjustment, and recommended books on religion.

While it is too soon to tell exactly what long-range benefits will accrue to Allen and his classmates, this much is already evident: interest, as judged by attendance and class growth, is unusually high, and the dropout rate is less than 10 per cent. This figure becomes significant when we compare it with the many times higher dropout rate of the average religious education program. Although the program has been in operation only about seven years, the number of boys and girls who graduate from high school and go off to college or start families of their own but who maintain an active membership in the church is phenomenal. Phenomenal, too, is the number who are preparing for some church-related profession. But most important of all, Allen has found a satisfying and secure faith in God and a challenging reason for being.

Obviously, the special religious education program for gifted children in Allen's church will not meet the requirements of every church. Some churches and synagogues, because of creed or tradition, will find such an approach to religion unacceptable, and smaller congregations will find it impractical.

Let us now consider the case of a gifted lad of eleven. Ray is a member of a small and quite conservative church. He has been attending church school all his life. Because he was in the fifth grade in school, he was placed in a class of juniors, many of whom had attended church school only a year or two, some even less. Although he had an unusually able teacher, Ray soon became bored. His parents found it increasingly difficult to get him to go, and when he did go he created confusion in the class. It soon became evident that such a situation could not continue. Ray was becoming resentful and rebellious, and the class was kept in an uproar. The teacher threatened to resign unless Ray was either removed or squelched.

Ray's mother, a public school teacher with some knowledge of the characteristics and problems of gifted children, suggested to the religious education director and the pastor that Ray be moved to the junior high class, a promotion of two years. The first reaction was that such a move was contrary to all orthodox church school rules and that it could create a dangerous precedent which might end in total confusion. But since either a boy or a teacher was to be lost, the decision was made to try it. Ray is large for his age and fits nicely in the older class. But what is more important, he is again happy in church school. As this account is written, this church is seriously considering making knowledge and ability, rather than class grade in school, the criterion for all promotion in the church school. No doubt the new system will create some problems, but it seems like one way to help the gifted child in the small church.

The only other church that we have been able to find which is trying to give gifted children some special help with religion is large and also conservative in belief. For their gifted boys and girls special classes have been formed within the departments of juniors and intermediates, grades four through nine. The children are carefully selected on the basis of observation by the teachers and the church school superintendent, who is also the superintendent of a large public school system, and placed in the special classes without the knowledge of either the pupils or their parents. Withholding this information was done in an attempt to escape criticism from other children and their parents, although one wonders how effectively this accomplishes that purpose. Curriculum materials which were prepared for senior high pupils are used in these special classes and adapted by the teachers for each class. Teachers are carefully chosen for their ability to stimulate interest and to lead the students to discuss their concerns and apply their religion to modern living. Interest, regularity of attendance, and numerical growth of these special classes are unusually high in comparison with the other classes of this church.

Love and Understanding

Walter is a brilliant young man, a clergyman, and president of a rapidly growing church-related college. He was brought up in a fundamentalist faith, but few things bothered him until he took a biology course in high school. Then, in swift succession, his mother died and a man he greatly admired was convicted of grand larceny. The bottom fell out of his religious beliefs. No end of serious questions filled his mind until he had about decided that God was a myth and the Bible a fairy tale.

Fortunately, however, Walter had a wise and understanding father, who himself had found a sound religious faith that left room for a few unanswered questions. He was convinced that faith has no magical hocus-pocus to solve all our problems, nor is it a guarantee of goodness. There are many things that one can never fully understand. What we call "truth" is relative—it is only the best answer that we have today, and it may well change tomorrow. If it has any validity for us it is because we dared to examine it and still found it true. He believed that one can hardly "save the soul" at the expense of intellectual integrity. But above all, he understood to a great degree how the highly intelligent mind of a boy like Walter could be filled with doubts and questions that needed rational consideration.

Walter's father was a clergyman who was Walter's religious teacher at church as well as at home. By means of his own rational thinking and teaching, plus his accepting understanding of gifted children, he was able to guide Walter in finding a satisfying faith.

From the study of Allen, Raymond, and Walter, and many other gifted persons like them, a logical and rather well defined pattern emerges which seems to avoid many of the frustrating and baffling conflicts inherent in the usual religious learning situation for gifted children. Basic to this pattern are the love and understanding exhibited by Walter's father.

The very best foundation upon which to build a strong religious faith is love—loving and being loved. The gifted child's mind soon reaches out into the unknown with a sense of awe and wonder. He may want some scientific and practical answers before he can understand them. Too, he must come to understand that there are some questions that cannot be answered yet. But *now* he can understand love. Loving and being loved are the most real things in his young life—they produce observable results in his world. However, no amount of words or gifts will substitute for the real thing. All children are sensitive in this matter, gifted children especially so.

Love is the very cornerstone of health from a psychological point of view. Both from a romantic and practical standpoint, real love is not "blind"—it is understanding. So many gifted children are permanently injured because they are not understood—they are round pegs pushed into square holes.

Understanding and love bring acceptance by both mind and emotions. It is often not easy to accept without some crippling reservation a child who is different, and the gifted child often seems to be a maverick. *But he must be accepted and feel accepted.* Loving guidance, not change or remodeling, is the aim. From a religious perspective this often is a most difficult task.

Help Him to Accept Himself

Usually, the child who is loved and accepted will love and accept himself. Since the gifted child is unusually perceptive, he will soon note that his interests and ways of thinking and reaction are different. Not infrequently he will be rejected by his playmates and fellow pupils; at the least, they will tease him about his strange (to them) interests. Unless he has support from adults who accept his different behavior and who help him to understand how and why he tends to act differently, he may not be able to accept himself. The result will be either withdrawal from social contact with other children or an attempt to repress his characteristics of giftedness. A very frequent form of this reaction is demonstrated by the underachiever who seeks conformity in his school work by studying only enough to get by.

Since many religious groups set up rather rigid standards for belief and behavior, the gifted child will be under extreme pressure to conform. Something is bound to give, and it is usually the gifted child. Of the many possible and unfortunate reactions mentioned in the previous chapter, unacceptance of self figures prominently. It should be obvious that understanding and accepting the gifted child for what he is, and thereby helping him to understand and accept himself, will benefit not only the child, but also the home, church, and society.

Encourage Him to Ask Questions

In most cases, the problems of gifted children with religion will find expression in questions, disturbing questions—that is, if asking questions has not been discouraged or penalized. This is an unexcelled and often overlooked opportunity to guide the child in his religious concepts and beliefs. As a rule, gifted children do not ask questions to get attention—they really want to know. And they want to know *why* even more than *what*. So, when your child asks questions, and he will ask them more frequently and with more seriousness the more gifted he is, you can to an unbelievable degree help him to build a sturdy faith for himself by helping him find adequate answers to them.

In order to do this, keep a few *dont's* in mind. When he asks questions that you cannot answer don't be afraid to say, "I do not know, but I will help you to find the answer." Don't feel irritated or insulted if he seems to know more about some things than you do; he very well may, but you know things which he does not know. Don't try to tell him what to believe without telling him why he should accept it as true. Perhaps it would be even better to suggest a number of possibilities and allow him to make his own choice of beliefs. Don't try to force him to accept vague generalities and flat dogmas as "truth." Don't try to form conclusions for him; help him to come to his own. Don't be afraid to help him understand that for many things we do not yet have the answers, but don't act shocked or cause him to feel that he is a "bad boy" because he asks shocking questions or doubts some fundamental beliefs.

Susan had a pet that she loved very much. One day it died rather suddenly. Her reaction was sorrowful anger: "I hate God! Why did he have to take my cat to heaven?" Although her mother was quite shocked at Susan's vehemence, she managed to react with less than the turmoil she experienced. She said, "I know you feel very angry now, but you will feel better in a day or two." She then had an opportunity to explain many things about death and God that the more usual reaction of shame and horror would have made impossible.

Find Adequate Answers

Some of the first questions the gifted child will ask are those which concern life and death. His inquisitive mind wants answers to questions about human existence, such as: Where did he come from? Where will he go after he dies? Is there a heaven? A hell? Why do we have to die? Where did the world come from? What is life? What is the purpose of life? These are fundamentally religious questions, but quite general. As he grows older, the questions will become more specific. If he has been taught Bible stories, he may ask if the Bible is true. Are the miracles true? Did God create the world and life as the Bible says? But science seems to tell another story. Which to believe?

During adolescence, the questions will become more complex and will be concerned with more involved theological concepts. What is God really like? Does he really exist? What do we mean by the Trinity? Atonement? Why did Christ have to die? Is man really depraved?

It is not the purpose of this book to suggest answers to these questions. To do so would be contrary to what we have been saying all along—that you and the gifted child must find answers that meet *his* needs. But there are several guiding principles to help you find some answers.

First, forget what you have heard or been told. Far too much of religious belief (and any other matter) consists of hearsay. Examine the facts insofar as facts are available. Consider every side of the question, for many questions have at least five or six sides. Read everything you can find on the subject, and from all points of view. When the Bible is questioned, remember that it is not a scientific treatise—its scientific knowledge is based on what was believed to be true at the time it was written.

It would be well in any consideration to remember that truth, even in its best sense, is relative. What we accept as fact today may well be fancy tomorrow. Furthermore, there are many questions for which we now have no answers. Do not be afraid to admit this to yourself and to the gifted child.

After careful consideration and examination, guide the child to form the conclusion that satisfies his own mind. Questions indicate interest, interest that should be encouraged by a frank willingness to face the facts. The gifted, creative child is never satisfied with rigid dogmas and ready-made answers. It is well that this is so—this mind may be the one that later finds a new theological truth or unlocks a long-sought-for secret of nature.

Resolve Contradictions

The keen observance and the logical manner of thinking of the gifted child makes inconsistencies and contradictions of primary concern to him. This is especially true concerning what people profess and what they live. While the injustices and inconsistencies in the world generally will trouble the gifted child, what matters most to him is what adults close to him do, compared to what they "preach."

He may reason that injustice and contradictions between ideals and practice result from the fact that no human being is perfect and that society is an accumulation of all of man's imperfections. We get into trouble when we suggest that religion is a cure-all for the ills of man and his world. At best, it is a set of ideals which we imperfectly seek as goals. It is not, and never was, a guarantee of goodness. If he is taught from this frame of reference, the gifted child may be spared the shattering experience of disillusionment when he faces inconsistencies in the conduct of someone he respects.

This is not to say that you ought not do your very best to live what you teach. If you profess love and kindness but instead are always critical and faultfinding, the child will soon adopt a negative feeling for what you profess, if not for you. In his mind he will say to himself, "This is not for me. I will have none of it." And nothing you can do will change his mind.

Begin to Help Him Early

One of the most harmful practices of some faiths is that of waiting until a child reaches the chronological age of twelve before teaching the basic religious doctrines and beliefs. Before that time, the practice dictates, tell him Bible stories and have him memorize easy portions of Scriptures. Tell him to love his neighbor, be kind, and say a prayer. But do not confuse him with anything more complex (or interesting).

This may be an excellent practice for the average child, but the gifted child needs and wants to know sooner. At least by the time a child reaches the *mental age* of about twelve, he is ready for deeper spiritual truths and concepts. This means that a child with an IQ of 150 would be ready by at least eight years of age and the bright child with 120 IQ by the time he is ten, both long before some religious groups consider it proper instruction.

It should be obvious that gifted children need to be taught creeds and doctrines of their religion as soon as they indicate an interest, rather than the arbitrary chronological age of twelve. The parents and teachers who watch for signs of interest will be alert, especially to the kinds of questions the child raises and the comments he makes. This is not to say that the more formal religious instruction in a pastor's or rabbi's class or catechism need be disrupted or its timetable rearranged. It is to say, however, that these talented children can and should be guided and instructed in the deeper matters of religion in the home and in the religious group by using methods and techniques suggested elsewhere in this chapter and in following chapters.

Another matter which is often neglected until it grows into a deep-seated problem is the gifted child's tendency to self-criticism and moral anxiety at an earlier age than most parents and teachers realize. Adults who are aware of this tendency can guide and encourage him. There is no sharp line of division between this characteristic and his sensitivity to injustices in society, but there is the addition of personal responsibility. He sets high standards not only for others, but for himself. Any sense of personal failure creates moral anxiety and guilt. All the understanding and wisdom you possess are required here, and early.

Consider the Whole Person

The gifted child has interests seemingly without religious significance. A generally accepted concept of personality is that a child is a whole person, that all his interests and activities are interrelated and must be integrated. To treat him as gifted in one setting and not in another would do irreparable harm. Encourage his giftedness in the home setting as well as in the religious setting, and of course there are many points at which they overlap.

1. Let him explore and initiate activities and hobbies, whether they are directly related to religion or not. Help him to develop these interests, but do not try to direct them. The interests of gifted chldren are extremely wide and varied. Do not discourage him unless they are harmful to him or others. Take him on field trips and excursions. Museums of all types seem to have a particular fascination. Interviews disclose that some of the most pleasant memories of church school held by some (far too few) gifted adults were the excursions and field trips they made as children. Parties seem to have little impression. The parent and the teacher who sincerely want to help the gifted child will engage in more activities of the excursion and field trip type.

2. The gifted child likes to read. Encourage this trait. Help him select challenging books, stories, biographies, and even theological works for older children. But be doubly sure that the religious books chosen are of high caliber— that the picture of life they present is sound and not overly simple and "good." Truly fanciful tales, some comic books, and science fiction are enjoyed, as are far more difficult works of nonfiction.

3. Encourage the gifted child to play with other children. Not infrequently he will become so engrossed in his own interests that he tends to neglect social contacts. Sometimes this occurs because he feels different or misunderstood, or to escape teasing, but more often he has no time for social activities. In such a case encouragement and social planning are necessary. Membership and participation in children's clubs, YMHA, YMCA, CYO, or YWCA, or youth organizations such as Brownies, Scouts, and religious fellowships are extremely valuable. Gifted children have a special need to learn the rules of the game, and to respect others and their rights. They may tend to be quite intolerant of those less gifted than they. They tend to assume positions of leadership, sometimes even to the point of usurpation. Patience and understanding of those less able should be taught, and an attitude of helpful sharing can be pointed out as more effective than domination. Such stewardship of their gifts is learned through loving and understanding guidance.

4. Resist the tendency to boast about the gifted child. He very likely will get better grades in school, learn faster, have more interests, find more advanced hobbies, and be a stronger leader than his peers. But vaunted pride and bragging comments can lead only to disaster of one kind or another. The child may either be embarrassed or he may become vain and snobbish. Love him no more and no less than your other children. He needs approval for genuine accomplishment, but let it not be excessive or to the disadvantage of other children. He is not the center of the universe. Others have talent, too, perhaps of a different sort, and he should respect them.

Whether he accomplishes little or much, your main interest should be that he becomes the best person he is capable of becoming. Sometimes expectations are set too high, even for a gifted child, and he is pressured prematurely into advanced work or too much work. Some parents and some schools, instead of neglecting gifted children, penalize their brightness with too much to do.

Either extreme of expecting too much or too little is dangerous. Do not overschedule his time, or give him too many responsibilities. He needs some things for which he alone is responsible and he also needs some hard work, but he needs time to play and work on his hobbies. (This topic will be treated at some length in Chapter 10.) All work and no play may not only make gifted Jack a dull boy, but it may well make him a frustrated and rebellious person as well. Give him freedom to make mistakes—to spill milk and tear his trousers. This is a particularly important point in homes where religion is taken very seriously.

Encourage Special Talents

In most religious circles musical talent receives consideration and encouragement through rhythm bands, choirs, and orchestras, and, more commonly, through vocal and instrumental solo work. Many congregations have a highly trained staff of musicians and a minister of music, all of whom devote a great deal of time to developing the musical talent of the members.

However, children with specialized abilities other than music are not so fortunate. Gifts which could profitably be encouraged by more congregations are dramatic ability, talent in the graphic arts, public speaking, and certainly social and leadership ability. Since these do not fit as easily into the customary pattern of leadership as does music, they are usually neglected. But encouragement need not depend upon highly trained leaders or teachers. All that is necessary to start, at least, is someone with an interest in one of these areas and an interest in talented children. The obvious place to begin is in the religious education class. Initiate some really creative activities and projects, and later special classes, groups, or clubs could be organized.

The community-centered church or synagogue makes a convenient place for hobby clubs and special interest groups to meet. Amateur astronomy, photography, stamp or coin collecting, and woodworking are only a few of the activities that gifted children in the community may be interested in. Even such unlikely interests as "drag racing" might profit from the influence of a religious group. Recently, the Park Place Church of God in Anderson, Indiana, received national attention in *Hot Rod Magazine* because of the "Escorts," a hot rod club sponsored by the church and directed by one of its ministers.

Conclusions

The special religious education programs which we suggest for the home and the religious institution grow logically out of an extensive study of gifted children and religion. They are determined by the conflicts which affect gifted children in this particular area. Most of the suggestions made here do not involve major or drastic doctrinal, organizational, or curriculum changes. They have to do more with understanding the characteristics and needs of gifted children and with methods of meeting these needs. Most of them can be used within the framework of existing religious education programs, and any parent, or any congregation, can begin with some of the following summarized recommendations:

1. The parents, pastor or rabbi, religious education director and teachers should become familiar with the general characteristics of giftedness in children, as well as the special problems and needs.
2. The next step is to identify the bright and gifted children of the group, using the methods suggested earlier in this book.
3. The group will have to decide how it can—considering its size, equipment, resources, and teachers—best help its gifted children. In large groups acceleration with or without grouping may be the best answer. Enrichment of program and the encouraging of questions and discussion could be used in any situation.
4. Whatever method is used, capable and trained teachers are needed. Since finding and enlisting good teachers is always a vexing problem, the best possible use should be made of those available. Not every good teacher is

good for gifted children, and a poor teacher may be worse than none. (Of this matter more will be said in a later chapter.)

5. Consideration should be given to curriculum materials. Not every group will be able to prepare its own materials as did one of the churches we studied, but most groups can use advanced materials, creative activities that permit true self-expression and develop talent, and enrichment methods and materials. These include excursions and field trips, outside reading, hobbies, and guided (not dominated) discussion of searching questions without requiring pat answers based on inflexible dogmas. Avoid drill and repetitious techniques of teaching.

6. As an additional opportunity, some specialized activities or hobby clubs may be sponsored during the week.

7. The pastor or rabbi is in an unusually strategic position, provided he has some understanding of gifted children and their problems, to give extra attention to them. They may be interested in reading some of the more advanced books in his library. His counsel and encouragement may be just the thing needed to carry them through perplexing religious, social, or personal problems.

8. Some method of evaluation should be used to determine the effectiveness of a program for gifted and talented children. Up to now this is a greatly undeveloped area of religious education, but a check on interest and dropout rates could be a good start for the average group. Of course, this will not work without accurate records and attendance follow-up—not so much to rekindle interest as to find out why interest was lost.

9. Of course, no program, however ambitious and pertinent, can meet all the religious needs of its gifted children by itself. It must have the help and cooperation of parents. It is, therefore, essential that parents know and understand their gifted children and their needs. The church or synagogue can help and be helped in this cooperative effort.

10. While there is much inertia, and many troublesome tra-

ditional attitudes and problems in the usual religious education situation may seem to make helpful changes improbable if not impossible, it *is* possible to make progress. Some parents and a few congregations have been able to do so. They have provided stimulating and challenging learning experiences for their gifted children.

Gifted and creative children must have a creative religion. As an added dividend, it has been demonstrated that any program that is good for gifted children is good for all children.

6

"THE MOST VALUABLE ABILITY GIVEN TO MAN"

T<small>HIS</small> is an age of adventure, rapid change, and progress in which there are literally new worlds to conquer. At the same time we strive to maintain or extend a standard of living for all Americans which makes the lives of not-long-ago kings pale in comparison. It is probably the most religious age of man, at least since primitive times: church membership has never been higher, the Bible tops the best-seller lists, and religious articles and books abound. Yet it is also an age of fear, for over it all hangs the deathly pall of an atomic shroud. And it is an age of immorality and social injustice, as sex becomes a perverted pastime for many, race riots against race, crime multiplies, and, people—many people—are hungry. The challenge of our children's world demands concerns and abilities beyond those of any past generation.

Now, as if designed for this age, a new understanding of educational development gives us much higher hopes and estimates of human potential than we have ever guessed were possible. Recent research concerning the nature of creativity and characteristics of creative children and adults indicates that we have been largely overlooking what Paul Witty calls "the most valuable ability given to man."

Perhaps the principle should be restated: When we speak of creativity we are not referring to a gift apart from intellectual giftedness, but rather we are describing one aspect of giftedness which in some individuals has not been adequately developed or which has been effectively squelched. This ability, the ability to create, even more recent investigations are disclosing, has such tremendous implications for the teaching of moral and spiritual values (religion) as to stagger the imagination.

An Acute Sense of Morality

It is both profoundly disturbing and sternly challenging to learn that children whose creative abilities have been well developed, or which have not been suppressed, hold and practice extremely high standards of moral and ethical conduct, motivated by a strong sense of inner-directed integrity. Their imagination and free-ranging intelligence, guided by a strong sensitivity, help them to be far more sympathetic and empathic-able to see another's world as if it were their own, than are those whose creative ability has been suppressed or undeveloped. It is as if God, indeed, had "written His words upon their hearts."

These are the startling findings of such authorities as Elizabeth Drews, Abraham Maslow, and Getzels and Jackson. Recent investigations by this writer confirm their conclusions. When two groups of very able children—matched for background, ability, sex, and age, but differing strongly in creative ability—were asked to make three wishes for anything they wanted most, the creative group twelve to one made unselfish wishes as compared to selfish wishes of the children whose creativity was underdeveloped.

Other characteristics of this creative group include keen awareness of reality within and without themselves, an autonomy that asserts itself in original and unique approaches to problems, and the courage to act on inner convictions in spite of group pressures. They are deeply religious in a searching and reinterpreting sense. They have the courage to befriend their odd and often unaccepted classmates, even if so doing results in their own unpopularity. Frequently these children are more socially concerned and helpful than they are sociable—they may not be socially "well adjusted."

Other studies, including those by Getzels and Jackson, find that the children whose creative ability has been highly developed differ almost diametrically from those children whose creativity has been undeveloped or crushed. The creative children prize such attitudes as social concern, postponement of satisfactions, autonomy, strong moral commitments, and often have less concern with high scholastic achievement (which in most cases is satisfactory but not outstanding). The high scholastic achievers, on the other hand, show greater conformity to socially accepted patterns of living, but at the same time they seem to have fewer moral scruples and demand more immediate satisfactions.

The author is now concluding a pilot study on creativity and motivation which strongly supports the hypothesis that high scholastic achievers tend to be motivated by a fear of failure and have a low risk preference scale. The highly creative group tend to be motivated by the satisfactions of success or anticipated success and have a substantially higher risk preference scale. The first group seem to need the security of high grades and rigorously high social conformity, but the creative group—being more autonomous—need less security in grades and social conformity. Our current educational and religious literature seems to suggest that greater welcome is given to the person who is "socially" adjusted than is given to the person with character. "If this is so, it calls for serious concern," Getzels and Jackson observe.

The really moral individual follows rules which make sense to him, and he modifies them intelligently according to differences in circumstances but rarely compromises his principle because someone "is looking" or "not looking." The socially "well adjusted" person tends to behave like the pet which stays off the sofa when his master is in the room, but hops on when his master is not present.

My studies and others have identified another group of gifted and creative individuals with strong autonomy and high moral standards who may tentatively appear to agree to certain social pressures in order to "get along" with others. They act with firm mental reservations purely for the sake of harmony. This acquiescence might be called a temporary "compromise" which they hope in the long run will accomplish more than outright opposition. But they retain their basic convictions and values which they will put into action when it is more feasible and success is more probable. This does not mean that they act hypocritically or that they adopt lesser values; it is more an abstention of voiced opposition or overt action until a more opportune time.

Plainly this is not to suggest that development of creative talent in gifted children is some magical cure-all for our social ills. Nevertheless, this aspect of creativity should deserve far more serious consideration than it now appears to be receiving. What evidence we now have seems to indicate that any educational system or teaching method that tends to stifle creativity by authoritarian methods of learning, or which submerges originality in a sea of social or religious conformity in the classroom —secular or religious—tends to foster moral rebellion, ethical dependence, or the superficial cloak of externally motivated moral conformity. On the other hand, individuals with well developed creativeness seem to possess the kind of social conscience, ethical behavior, and moral integrity that characterize the stated objectives of secular and religious education. May we never forget that man is no mechanical automaton, nor is he of the genus *Thaumetopoea processionea* (processionary caterpillar). He has the driving spark of creativity.

Only a generation ago, the great plea of those concerned with freedom and social conscience was that unfettered individualism must be curbed for the sake of society as a whole. *Time* magazine a few years ago said:

Today's champions of the individual do not worry about religious persecution but about religious blandness, not about outright tyranny but about creeping collectivism, not about economic exploitation but blind and well-paid loyalty to one's job. In short the freedom that is threatened is the freedom of the individual to be fully himself.[2]

Whatever else releasing creative talent in gifted children may accomplish, it most certainly will free these individuals to be themselves. No tyranny or collectivism can enslave the truly creative person.

[2] "Lincoln and Modern America," *Time,* May 10, 1963, p. 24.

Therefore, a creative education which prizes a child's individuality and which develops to the uttermost his creative ability—as well as his verbal and academic potential and his knowledge of creeds and doctrines—is a must if the child "grows as he be" and fits into our highly technological culture. Yet he must become a person with a highly sensitive and inner-directed social conscience, with a sense of moral values, or all else is valueless. It necessarily follows, then, that *how* a child is taught is as important as *what* he is taught. No amount of knowledge or variety of skills, however important they are, can make up for lack of the ability to create, enjoy life, and contribute to the welfare of mankind.

Why We Are Concerned

The overriding fact that children with well developed creativity are, to put it simply, more truly religious, gives us cause to be vitally concerned. After Paul Witty stated that "creativity is the most valuable ability given to man," he added this distressing comment: "We are wasting this talent. As a matter of fact, by our widely used tests of ability and educational methods, we are systematically sifting out creative talent and denying its development."

Never has there been more for the creatively talented man to do. Our families, our churches, our nation, and our world need the creative thinker, the innovator, the individual who has different ideas and at the same time a highly developed sense of moral and spiritual values. But for the most part in the religious setting and in the home, creative development at best is left to chance—in most cases we could hardly do a more effective job of destroying it if we tried, squelching it early in life by popular but nonactive social and educational practices. And in the religious group we have unwittingly been destroying what we have been trying hardest to accomplish, the development of inner-directed moral and spiritual values.

Here are some specific reasons why we should be concerned about the development of children's creative talent:

1. Unless creative ability is identified and encouraged *early* in the life of a child, the probability is that he will sacrifice his divergency and creativity for nonproductive conformity. For years students of creativity have noticed a decided drop in curiosity and creative activity in gifted children soon after entering school. It has always been assumed that this decline was a purely developmental phenomena. Torrance especially refuses to accept this explanation, but insists that it is due to the child's response to peer, parent, and teacher pressures to conform. There is no disagreement among authorities that conformity and creativity cancel each other out.

2. Recent and ongoing studies show that even traditional skills and knowledge can be taught more economically and effectively when creative abilities are utilized in their learning. This involves exploratory, manipulative activities in which divergent thinking is often present. Learning and thinking are not highly formulated and stylized, but often follow unconventional interests and patterns. Many schools and especially many religious groups discourage or even forbid such methods of learning. At the same time other schools place such heavy emphasis upon "group" and "social" activities that they submerge the individual and whatever creative thinking or learning he may develop. Nothing stifles creative learning as thoroughly as pressure to conform to group standards. Apparently the learning processes flourish best in the truly creative environment, described as that situation in which . . . "children are permitted and encouraged to explore, solve problems, figure things out, think things through for themselves . . . arriving at an insight, a solution, and maybe developing creativity. Then learning also is more effective."

A Further Definition of Creativity

In addition to the description given of creativity in Chapter 3 as an aspect of giftedness, some further definition should be helpful. Most authorities agree that creativity in one form or another is universal among children, but there is no universal agreement as to what creative ability is or what the best way may be to identify it. One of the best definitions that this writer has found is stated by Andrews:

Creativity is uniquely human. It is a quality of living; a special human awareness of seeing, feeling, hearing, and sensing what others may not. Creativity is the going beyond of what one at the moment seems to know or sense. This individualistic human quality—creativity—makes it possible for one to: make choices, act independently, discover new possibilities, see some new relationships, look for the unexpected, try something in a different way, take chances without knowing the outcome, reconstruct old ideas and associations, and then focus on new alternatives. Creativity is a dynamic force or power, an inherent part of everyone's make-up which can be encouraged, extended, and expressed.[3]

A popular conception limits creativity to abilities in certain specific areas such as art, writing, or music. Hopefully, this definition is being replaced by the concept that creativity is evident in all areas of expression. More often than not, when fully developed creative ability appears to be generic, that is, it is a general ability which affects all the areas of living. A classic example was the very versatile Leonardo da Vinci.

Torrance, Getzels, and Jackson, who emphasize the basic importance of creative thinking, also take the viewpoint that creativity is looking at anything and everything in ways that are different and divergent in concepts and conclusions. They do not assume that this creative type of intellectual ability is characteristic only of persons judged to be creative in the artistic or scientific sense. Rather, they start with the assumption that these creative abilities are found to some extent *in all persons*—children and adults, sculptors and astronomers, architects and bricklayers, artisans and salespeople, reformers, rabbis, and ministers. They believe that there is a high positive correlation between creative thinking and accomplishment in any creative endeavor.

[3] Gladys Andrews, "Releasing Creativity-Extending Curriculum Opportunities," *Curriculum for Today's Boys and Girls,* ed. Robert S. Fleming (Columbus, Ohio: Charles E. Merrill Books, Inc., 1963), p. 403. Used by permission of publisher.

There is general agreement that creative talent expresses it-self by producing something—an idea, a composition of music or words, a picture, a building, a social or religious concept—which is essentially one's own, the production of an individual. The parts may be old and the methods long used, but creative talent adds something that is distinctively characteristic of the producer.

Not infrequently we find critical thinking, problem-solving, and creative thinking lumped together almost as if they were one and the same thing. An analysis of the learning processes involved show many common elements in these mental activities. There is no doubt that all three are involved in creative production; however, there are distinctions. Creative thinking is the production of new ideas, while critical thinking involves our reaction to the ideas of others or to our own previous ideas. Problem-solving is more objective, more directed toward some goal which is usually external, and more consonant with the facts. Creative thinking is usually more personal, concerned about others, and less fixed by circumstances.

Can Creativity Be Taught?

Is creativity an inherent ability genetically acquired or de-termined by heredity, or is it a product of environment? Can it be taught? There is general agreement that creativity can be developed and expressed by children and adults. There is also general agreement that creative ability, except in unusual cases, can all too easily be squelched and destroyed.

All creative activity is to a great extent exploratory and di-vergent with a pronounced amount of risk. Highly conforming individuals or insecure persons do not as a rule express their creative talent. Present also in creative endeavor is what may be called a "fire in one's bones," or a "thorn in the flesh"—a disturbing inner tension which causes one to do something or attempt to do something creative. F. S. C. Northrop goes so far as to say that no one is a creative thinker unless he is disturbed by something. The people who are satisfied and complacent, or who are fearful, do no creative thinking. Sensitivity to a disturbance or problem produces creative thinking as one stays with it, analyzes it, and comes up with a speculative hypothesis for a solution. This speculative leap into the dark is the essence of creative thinking which seeks a possible solution to the problem that causes the inner tension, or "fire in one's bones."

This implies a high degree of personal involvement which, as a matter of fact, is so important that a recent study of graduate students doing research in college indicates that only those who demonstrated *emotional involvement* in graduate research produced any significant creative research later.

It is clear that the creative thinker brings into the creative situation certain elements that obviously cannot be taught but which inhere in his individuality. But at the same time he brings attitudes, skills, and methods which just as obviously can be taught and developed.

Factors Which Tend to Obscure Creativity

One of the most significant and disturbing discoveries of recent studies is that creative talent more often than not is obscured by certain characteristics of the creative person, plus other factors operating in the average educational situation at home, school, synagogue, or church. The most important obscurational factors are these:

1. There is no general correlation between creative talent and the score a child makes on an intelligence test, nor does high academic ability necessarily indicate high creative ability. In other words, tests of intelligence as they are now constituted do not test the ability to be creative. Apparently there are other factors inherent in the creative process. However, most creative children and adults have above average intelligence, but not generally in the very high range. Witty stated that a high IQ is excellent background, and the creative person with a high IQ probably is more creative than the creative person with a low IQ. But any attempt to assess creative talent by means of current tests of intelligence will fail.

2. Recent studies find a small but consistently significant negative correlation between grades and creative ability. The creative pupil is not likely to be a straight A nor even an A and B student; more than likely he will fall into the B or C category. A recent study disclosed that of all professions in college, research scientists and architects had the lowest grade point averages. But more significantly, most of these creative adults would not have been admitted into colleges today with the strong emphasis on academic achievement. As it was, many of them found it extremely difficult to maintain a grade average sufficiently high to stay in college long enough to graduate.

3. Creative individuals are basically nonconformists as contrasted to many high academic achievers who are conformists of a high order. The creative thinker is usually on his own, exerts autonomy of mind, and displays resistance to group pressures. The creative child will do one of two things: 1) He will repress and squelch his creativity, or 2) he will learn to handle his drive to creativeness along with the tensions that come from being many times a minority of one. Unfortunately, most creative children quickly learn that it is far easier to conform, easier to hide their divergency and originality than to stand alone. This is especially true in the home, school, or religious group where conformity is too much prized and divergency is penalized.

4. Creative children are often hard to live with. They may not be well-rounded. Their very divergency makes them misfits. They may lack in some particular phase of development, and their verbal abilities may be below average. These children detest rote learning, memorizing, and drill, preferring to "figure it out" or refer to a standard reference or textbook.

5. Some types of curriculum tend to obscure creative talent. Obviously, the authoritarian, teacher-dominated, subject-centered curriculum allows little opportunity for creative expression or evaluation. Likewise, the highly socialized and extremely group-centered learning situ-

ation tends to submerge the creative abilities of children. These children prefer to learn on their own with a minimum of guidance or group dynamics. Many teachers are slow to recognize this fact, assuming that children cannot learn on their own. Other teachers seem to believe that the only worthwhile learning takes place in group participation and committees.

Furthermore, many schools, including those in church and synagogue, provide for creative expression only in some specialized form such as art or music. Other types of creative expression and activity, such as creative thinking and investigation, are unfortunately overlooked. There is as yet no valid information which lets us assume that creative expression in music will produce a creative writer, or that creative activity with a paintbrush will develop a creative clergyman or scientist. Rather, it now seems that a general creative atmosphere in the classroom which treats all learning and all experiences creatively is by far the best environment for releasing and developing creative talent. Of this subject more will be said in Chapter 7.

6. Although highly gifted creative children are often difficult to recognize as such, even more so is the average creative child. Not always do the ideas of creative children have merit, nor do their solutions seem practical, nor are their contributions valuable. They may appear to be only misfits with strange and silly ideas, or perhaps misbehaving mischief-makers who always want to do things their own way. Their teachers and their peers often feel that the creative child just does not belong in the average classroom and that he is a neurotic who needs help to adjust. These and other factors operate in most classrooms to obscure the creative talent of children, and the pressures against divergency are subtle and powerful. Torrance says, "In no group studied thus far have we failed to find relatively clear evidence of pressures against the most creative members of the group." Nevertheless, creativity *can be identified* by those who care enough to do so.

How to Identify Creative Talent

Since it will be some time before existing tests of creative ability will be in common use and since it may not always be practical or advisable—especially in the religious setting—to use formal tests to measure creative talent, some nontest criteria of evaluation may be helpful. The following is a list of identifying characteristics of creative children compiled by this writer from various sources. The creative child:

1. Does creative things. Plainly the child who can and does create is creative. However, we should not overlook the fact that the created product or idea may or may not be practical or valuable. Some children may be creative in lies or mischief. Torrance tells of one of the most creative children he has ever discovered whose first evidence of originality was in the lies he told.

2. Exhibits a need to know more about himself and his environment. There usually is a "going beyond" quality in the creative child's curiosity and activity.

3. Scans his surroundings with new ways of looking, seeking new experiences. He uses all his senses in observing.

4. Reacts positively to new, strange, incongruous or mysterious elements in his environment by moving toward them and manipulating them. This manipulative curiosity is so annoying that it is usually quickly squelched or penalized.

5. Persists in examining and exploring interesting stimuli in order to know more about them.

6. Has a remarkable sense of humor that is more subtle than broad and slapstick.

7. Is often a "loner" who refuses to participate, or does so reluctantly, in group activities. He often refuses to join the Scouts, or the youth group at synagogue or church. He may have few friends, and he may prefer to work on projects by himself.

8. Has a good imagination and may be a daydreamer

lost in his own thoughts. He is a "what-if?" child and enjoys pretending.

9. Is forgetful and absentminded. His mind seems to wander.

10. May get good grades in only one or two subjects such as science, art, music, or mathematics. In the religious group he may seem interested in certain aspects of religion or certain doctrines.

11. Gives "off-beat" or unusual answers to questions, attemps unorthodox solutions to problems, and has strange ways of doing common things.

12. Is often unusually inner-directed and seems not to be bothered, and often is not, about the acceptance of others. He does not mind the consequences of appearing to be different from others. His conscience is highly developed. Being right within himself is most important. This characteristic, an extremely sensitive evaluation of creative development, is frequently stifled by parent, teacher, and peer pressures.

13. Can usually occupy his time by his own pursuits and hobbies without overt stimulation.

14. Is an experimenter and explorer who is not afraid to try new things. He finds unusual uses for his toys, or may be able to amuse himself with simple things which would not interest less creative children. He sometimes does not follow directions well. He reconstructs and rebuilds.

15. Is irritated and bored by the routine and the obvious, prefers complex and unusual ideas, and may be able to handle more than one at the same time.

16. Is a "window-watcher" who somehow manages to keep up with his class and may appear to be loafing or daydreaming while he is actually thinking or paying attention. (Let every teacher remember this!)

17. Has a sensitivity to problems and can seem to "smell them out" and define them clearly while others less creative may overlook them.

18. Becomes emotionally involved with tasks and causes that catch his fancy and interest. He finds it difficult to re-

main objective in creative activities or about social and
religious problems.

19. Has a great amount of flexibility and persistence. If he
cannot do it one way, he will keep trying other ways until he succeeds or is satisfied that it cannot be done.

20. Has an unusual amount of self-confidence and self-
reliance without arrogance. He tends not to be self-
righteous.

A number of more formal and structured nontest ways of
finding creative ability may be suggested. One of the most obvious is the assignment at home or in the religious group of activities which require creative responses. Autobiographies and
interest checklists may also be used, but their construction and
use require a great deal of knowledge and creativity on the part
of the teacher.

These criteria are not to be used as absolute measuring sticks;
they are indicators and indicators only. *There is no such child
as a typically creative child.* Not all children have all of these
characteristics and not to the same degree. But all children have
some of them to some degree, as all children are to some degree creative. One use of the above list would be as a measuring
stick or method of evaluation of creative development and progress in children. It could obviously be used to evaluate creative
teaching in any classroom or to test creative encouragement in
the home.

Some children who are potentially quite creative may no
longer exhibit any of these characteristics because their creativity
has been successfully stifled. They have become "well adjusted"
and "socialized" conforming members of their group.

7

CREATIVE TEACHING OF RELIGION
FOR GIFTED CHILDREN

NUMEROUS recent studies confirm what has long been suspected—*the single most important factor in learning is the teacher*. We can do all we can about curriculum and methods and resources and administrational devices and special programs, but a good teacher is far and away the most urgent requirement for the social, religious, and educational development of children. This is not to say that these other factors are not important; they are. A good teacher can do a better job with better tools, but no tool will work itself.

When we go on to say that gifted children require the best teachers available, we are not saying that average children do not need good teachers. We are saying, however, that the challenge and the potential are greater with gifted children. Their teachers not only need innate ability and whatever general training they can obtain in subject matter and methods, but also some special instruction and understanding of what is involved in teaching gifted children.

Just recently a public school teacher told of a meeting she had attended in which homogeneous grouping for gifted children was discussed. When the matter of teachers for these special classes was considered, the principal of a large high school said, "Anyone can teach gifted children, but it takes a really able teacher to teach slow learners."

He was right on the last count, but so wrong on the first. To those who understand gifted children and their special education needs, this was an incredible attitude. But it does express a popular attitude prevalent even yet among some educators, that "genius will out."

Gifted children in public schools or in schools of religion need able teachers with special interests and abilities. Not every able teacher can be an effective teacher of slow learners or of gifted children. Rather belatedly we are learning that teaching the gifted means much more than exposing the highly intelligent child to more work more quickly. We are coming to the incontrovertible conclusion that the gifted child follows a learning pattern quite different from the average child. Walter Barbe and Edward Frierson conclude, "If this is true, the teacher of the gifted child must not be satisfied only to teach more, or more rapidly, but must teach differently. Traditionally, the teacher has been concerned with the product of learning rather than the process, the possession of knowledge rather than the projection of knowledge. The process of learning is as important as the content and product."

Creative or Creedalized Religion?

Emphasis on content and product rather than on process is especially evident in religious education. Too much of religion is formalized and creedalized to the extent that it defies investigation. The goal seems to be that of turning out conformists, stereotypes of mass-produced believers whose religious concepts are "completed" and whose faith is "developed"—rather than individuals who can think creatively and who find a working, satisfying, and growing religious experience.

This common approach presents such knotty problems to the gifted mind that baffling frustration is inevitable. For a religious belief to be of real value to an individual it must grow out of the uniqueness of the person, together with all the circumstances of his life on the one hand and all the religious beliefs and events on the other. Unfortunately, we make an arbitrary distinction between "good" and "bad." If it is old and traditional it is good, but if it is new and different and creative, it is bad. This is a tragic delineation. Nevertheless, some doubtless will persist in making this judgment, for it is the difference between teaching which strives to produce a preconceived religious end-product and that which emphasizes the creative and never-ending process of learning and religious development.

This does not mean that there are no religious beliefs that are potentially constructive and others that are potentially destructive. When an individual is open to and aware of all the areas of his experiences, religious and personal, then what he develops and creates will tend to be constructive for both himself and others. But when he denies or represses areas of his experience, his resolutions and synthesis may well be pathological.

It is precisely at this point that much of religion and its methods of instruction tend to develop what it abhors, for it denies in practice the consideration of all areas of individual experience. It says, consider only those which seem to agree with stated creeds and dogmas, and forget those that seem to be in conflict. As a result, many of the outcomes and concepts are not constructive, but pathologically destructive to the individual.

There is no value in examining the motives of an individual who brings his thinking mind to bear on religious beliefs. We must face the fact that the gifted person thinks and creates primarily because it is satisfying to him, *and he can no more help his reaction than he can help that he thinks in the first place.* But an understanding teacher can help him to use this characteristic gift constructively.

The Role of the Teacher

Dr. Torrance tells this story: Once upon a time there was a monkey who could not climb trees but who could fly. The other monkeys laughed at him, teased him, and badgered him because he couldn't climb, but they gave him no credit at all for his unusual ability. Finally, when he was frightened out of his ability to fly, great relief came to him—the other monkeys no longer called him names or teased him.

The psychology of education has shown repeatedly that all

people tend to learn and develop along the lines that they find rewarding and satisfying. The religious institution for the most part has long rewarded conformity and penalized creativity. In my studies of the gifted child in church, I have been deeply impressed with this fact. I have been struck with even greater force by this needless tragedy as letters from many parents of gifted children come to me in response to my articles. Most of them can be briefly summed up in a few words: "My child hates church school! Why?"

The necessary role of the teacher of religion becomes increasingly clear—the nonconforming and creative thinker must be respected and rewarded. While this is especially true for all talented children, it is particularly true for boys. The thinking abilities of boys are increasingly superior to girls until about the third or fourth grade, or until ages nine or ten, when boys show a sharp drop in their creative abilities as they begin to lose the battle against conformity. This is true in public school, but is even more significant in religious education.

The problem of rewarding creative nonconformity is a most difficult one. There are no shortcuts in twelve easy lessons. But there are guidelines with which to start:

1. The first essential ingredient of effective teaching is a secure learning atmosphere. This has the highest priority, for without this basic and fundamental aspect of the learning environment none of the others function properly. Even more importantly, lack of this secure and warm learning atmosphere may destroy all the other necessary factors in learning, however good they may be in themselves. And the learning atmosphere is wholly within the control of the teacher.

    Under this category are such essentials as fairness, affection, respect, trust, freedom to speak without fear of censure, success rather than failure, reinforcement of learning, understanding and acceptance. Furthermore, this warm and secure atmosphere *must be perceived by the learner*. Real learning cannot take place without communication, real communication is impossible without rapport between teacher and pupil, and effective rapport is impossible without acceptance and affection.

It is sometimes assumed that this warm and secure learning environment is necessary only with small children. Recent studies, however, at the college level show conclusively that college students learn best, learn more, retain it longer, develop better understanding, and identify higher moral and spiritual values in an accepting, secure learning atmosphere in which they perceive the teacher as fair, understanding, and respectful. But let any teacher face a group of students with the attitude that he is going to show them how dumb they are and how learned he is, let him act and behave as if they were never or rarely to be trusted, let him act as if he did not fully accept or respect them or their ideas—and that teacher is through as an effective instructor.

2. The teacher must love his pupils more than he loves his subject matter or lesson material. Some teachers teach because they love children, while there are others who teach because they love their subject matter (they have an important lesson to teach). To whatever degree this is the case, the teacher who primarily loves children will be a better teacher than the one who is enamored with his subject matter (religion). The methods, attitudes, philosophy of education, and relationship of teacher to students will be almost diametrically opposed in the two extremes. Obviously there will be blending and overlapping, but one could plot a curve showing a positive relationship between pupil-centered teaching and effective learning and between subject-matter-centered teaching and lack of learning.

This is not to infer that a teacher who loves his children may not love his subject matter, or that a teacher who is deeply attached to his discipline may not be deeply attached to his pupils as well. Nevertheless, a good teacher is first of all a teacher who cares about his students and who secondly cares about his subject matter. How often in public school, college, or religious education we hear a statement such as this: "But I have to teach the lesson!" To a child- or person-centered teacher the person comes first, and the subject matter becomes merely the *means* to an end, not the end in itself. To paraphrase a statement of the Great Teacher, man was not made for subject matter, but subject matter was made for man.

3. It is important that the teacher of gifted children possess a basically strong personal faith that will withstand critical reexamination. Religious convictions are among the most intimate and personal beliefs one can have, and one cannot share them with others, or guide others in their own search for faith, without becoming personally involved. As a matter of fact, one cannot effectively teach children, gifted or not, without this involvement in the learning process. This of necessity includes evaluation of self and of one's beliefs as one evaluates the learner and his beliefs and guides him in the process of learning. In this process, new and perhaps conflicting ideas and concepts are bound to appear. They cannot be dismissed lightly and without consideration. To do so is to fall back into the error of traditionalism, which seems to say that if it is new and conflicting, reject it—it is bad. Therefore, the teacher of gifted children needs a tough and resilient faith with a personal capacity for religious growth in the continuing pursuit of knowledge.

4. While a trend to consider individual differences is beginning in a few congregations, too often the lessons and the teaching are the same for all pupils in any one group (or class) without taking into consideration differences either in ability or background. In creative teaching the lessons are adapted to each individual according to his needs, and with the gifted the direction of learning is largely determined by the pupil himself.

The teacher guides and directs learning, which may be in the direction of established concepts but may well be toward the discovery of novel facts and concepts. The absence of rigidity permits the assimilation into religious beliefs of new facts of physical science, sociology, and psychology, making an integrated rather than a conflicting set of convictions. This creative process is uniquely satisfying to the gifted person; its rewards are stimulating.

This is not to say that there are no bounds or goals in creative teaching of religion. It is to say that these bounds and aims are not fixed arbitrarily by the teacher or religious authority, and when we say this we realize that it amounts almost to heresy. Nevertheless, it must be said. It is the difference between a dead and destructive set of creeds and dogmas and a growing and creative faith. The direction and goals of process-oriented, or creative-oriented, teaching are determined by the spiritual, emotional, and intellectual needs of the learner, by his experiences, interests, characteristics, and resources. Again, the goal is determined by the needs and characteristics of the student, not by the teacher or religious authority. All great teachers have invariably used *truth* to meet the needs of *individuals*.

5. The foregoing philosophy implies a high quality of ingenuity and resourcefulness in the teacher of gifted children. He cannot rely on many of the prepared and predigested curriculum materials. Most of these are of little value for gifted children. Therefore, the methods and materials will of necessity grow out of the problem areas developed spontaneously in the classroom. While prepared materials may be of some help in suggesting starting points, they will need interpretation, revision, qualification, and possible rejection on the basis of suitability for his particular class.

This may suggest to some teachers that no preparation is necessary or possible, that he will have to "play it by ear" when he meets his class. On the contrary, preparation is most demanding, requiring a wide scope of knowledge and resources. Extensive reading is a must. He needs in addition a firsthand knowledge of people, pamphlets, books, visual aids, and possible field trips that may apply to the matter under consideration. In addition, he must be able to pull ideas and resources out of his sleeve, to "play it by ear" when the occasion demands.

6. No teacher of gifted children can be disrespectful of either the unusual questions or strange ideas of gifted children. More, though they may be disturbing in the extreme, the teacher should not show that he is disturbed. Some children may ask questions or throw out wild ideas just to get attention, but most children (gifted or not) ask questions because they want to know. If a child is respected and his ideas and questions are treated with respect, he will not need to seek attention. Nothing is more satisfying to a child who asks questions than to find answers. Nothing is more rewarding to a child who has an idea than to have others consider it.

This does not mean that questions should be answered immediately, although the need for an answer may be acknowledged quickly. Children can learn to enrich the period between questions and answers. They can learn the skills of inquiry, investigation, discussion, and give-and-take. They can learn to accept the questioning attitude without ready-made answers. Also, they can learn to understand that sometimes there are no answers—not yet, at least, to some questions.

The teacher of gifted children must be prepared for questions which he cannot answer, and for ideas that he may not understand. This is normal and desirable. When this happens, admit casually and frankly that you do not know. Do not feel ashamed or threatened. Instead, share the joy and adventure there is in seeking whatever is on the other side of the mountain. Stimulate questions and ideas, don't squelch them. Show your gifted children that their questions and ideas have value. Not infrequently teachers complain, "What you suggest is fine. I want my pupils to ask questions and share ideas, but I can't get them to talk. I have tried everything." Observation of these teachers in action discloses one or more of several reasons for nonparticipation of students:

a) The pupils do not actually have an opportunity to participate. The teacher may attempt to stimulate discussion briefly, but hurries on to continue his lecture. Or he may do it so infrequently that the children do not readily respond. A continuous atmosphere of freedom is essential.

b) Sometimes the teacher asks questions that can be answered yes or no, or they are "loaded," easily satisfied by pat answers.

c) In other cases students are afraid to share their ideas or doubts. They have been penalized, ridiculed, or have not been shown respect in class. It will take time to develop free discussion.

d) There are a few children who indicate a long background of having been squelched in one way or another. They are shy and retiring. It will take more than the usual amount of perserverance and understanding to help them express themselves freely in an accepting and secure learning atmosphere.

e) Then, of course, there are teachers who simply do not have the ability or the skill necessary to lead their pupils beyond the simplest level of learning.

All children, and especially the gifted, have strong curiosity and exploratory tendencies. The problem of those who teach religion to children is to keep it alive. One must constantly beware of the strong tendency in religion to say "This is it" rather than "Let's see if this is it." These are the areas in which satisfying rewards in learning have been denied to many children in the religious setting, but the gifted child has suffered most.

Should the Development of Creativity Be Left to Chance?

We dare not slight creativity as a central purpose of religious education—if the church and synagogue and all that they stand for are to escape becoming mere institutions, ineffectual in all their reasons for being. It has become the conviction of this writer that religious education should be concerned with the process of creativity as an all-encompassing attitude and atmosphere, affecting the entire religious education experience—rather than a specialized emphasis, concentrating on a few segments or areas of activity. To narrow its range, as in the latter case, may be to neglect or stifle creative response in other areas or as a basic attitude for living. Such a course would frustrate our reason for developing creativity early in children—namely, to help them develop into the persons God created them to be, realizing their fullest potential with its attendant personal satisfactions and contributing to society within a framework of creative moral and spiritual character of the highest order.

This approach to teaching religion is based upon four premises: First, all children are potentially creative to some degree. Second, creativity can be released and developed by the proper kind of learning experiences. Third, the most effective teaching is that which generates an all-pervading atmosphere of creative response for *all* the experiences and *every* concern of the individual. Fourth, the best possible kind of learning in all areas is that which is creative.

How to Release and Develop Creativity

Release and development of creativity denote action. In fact, the word *creativity* denotes action. Gladys Andrews describes creative activities:

... they involve try-exploring-seeking-extending-thinking-learning-identifying-interacting-helping-making-organizing-changing-discovering-evaluating-choosing-judging. They denote progressing, going ahead, going beyond, trying another way, becoming more aware, looking for alternatives. Creative action results in feelings of satisfaction, accomplishment, disappointment, discouragement, encouragement, frustration, spontaneity, and enthusiasm. . . . Creative action involves personally dealing with ideas, situation, hunches, which are *selected, organized, and translated or expressed in personal forms of communication.*[4]

[4] "Releasing Creativity-Extending Curriculum Opportunities," *Curriculum For Today's Boys and Girls,* ed. Robert S. Fleming (Columbus, Ohio: Charles E. Merrill Books, Inc., 1963), p. 405. Used by permission of publisher.

Involvement in creative action in the religious education setting takes a multitude of forms. There is no specific pattern. Therefore, we will be concerned here with general principles which can be applied to any form of creative ability or expression, but which will more importantly help to foster a creative atmosphere.

The following list of methods and approaches to the development of creative talent is compiled by this writer from a multitude of sources:

1. Exploration at any learning level is one of the best ways to get started, but this in itself is not enough. There needs to be a wide variety of opportunities for continued exploration, structured to some degree by careful planning, careful selection, and arrangement, and channeled according to age, needs, interests, and development.

   The discoveries of exploration then need to be used, tested and examined, interpreted, and expressed in meaningful forms such as a play, painting, project, story, social problem, getting along with others, or new ways of dealing with an old problem.

2. One mark of creative talent is what may be called self-starting ability. Not only should there be times of structured or directed exploration, there need to be also times of self-initiated exploration and activity. Most gifted children have a strong tendency in this direction; the problem of the teacher is to keep it alive. Periods of self-started learning are an important part of creative development. Studies of creative people disclose a significantly greater amount of independent study and a far less-structured training on the whole than that given less creative persons. The creative groups also showed a far lesser degree of authoritarian relationship with their teachers than the less creative groups. This will be hard for many teachers to accept. It is not the way it "always has been done."

3. Sensitivity to spontaneous situations and responses, or an event which captures the moment, is an important

part of developing creativity. Watchfulness for new ideas, for strange and different directions of interest, and for unexpected leads may be another way of putting it.

4. This sensitivity and watchfulness implies a high degree of flexibility, or adaptability, in order to capitalize upon the discovery of the moment. Use and adapt experiences while they are "red-hot." No teacher who is bound by some inflexible timetable, lesson plan, or preconception of what is supposed to happen can make use of the moment. Neither will he develop creative talent in his children, nor keep interest alive. As children become involved in discussing a current happening in which creative thinking and planning are going on, the value may be lost if they must wait for the "right" time.

5. A child needs imagery in order to go very far in realizing his creative potential; therefore, a creative situation provides a rich store of materials which enrich imagery. There is virtually no limit to the kinds of materials and situations which meet this need for stimulation. A partial list might start with the fact book of nature and run on through Bible stories, myths, folk tales, and fables of many countries. Ancient and modern paintings are valuable, too.

6. Creative children need time to think and daydream. This is some of the stuff from which creative ideas spring. In America it is almost illegal to be occupied with thinking and meditating—one must be visibly busy—and many teachers support this fallacy.

7. Establish a receptive atmosphere in which all children feel important, where strange ideas are valuable, unusual questions respected, and divergent responses encouraged. To express his creativity, a child must be freed from the immediate control of environmental rewards and punishments. Otherwise his efforts to conform to these pressures will block creative effort. This kind of nonevaluative atmosphere is not easy to produce. It takes time and patience. The teacher's attitude is of the

utmost importance. Signs of uncertainty, fear, and insecurity must be watched for carefully. Boys and girls need to learn that their ideas will not be laughed at or derided by their peers. Lifted eyebrows, the look of derision, giggles, punched ribs, or shrugged shoulders are to be strongly discouraged.

Some positive method of recognition and credit should be used to show children that their ideas and responses have merit whether or not they have any practical value. Acceptance and respect may be sufficient.

8. Prize rather than punish true individuality. Children really prize their individuality, and they must understand that the adults who guide them, and their peers, do also.

9. Expect noises.

10. While nonconformity and individuality are to be emphasized and prized, at the same time children need to learn to work together creatively in groups. One individual must not be allowed to impose his will upon the others. There must be opportunities for the group to discuss ideas, brainstorm, extend and develop ideas, and make appropriate choices. Ideas are helped to enlarge as a result of participation in cooperative groups.

There is a danger of group dominance when the group no longer serves the individual, but the individual serves the group. While his identity and creativity may be submerged in the mass, the group can and ought to serve a useful purpose in the development of creative talent.

11. It is important that every child have what Torrance calls a patron or sponsor. Society in general, and peers and many teachers in particular, are downright hostile to creative thinkers, especially when they are young. The creative person needs a relationship in which he feels safe. His patron or sponsor can provide a refuge, help him understand his divergence, let him express and communicate his ideas, see that his creative ideas are recognized and appreciated, and help others understand him.

Whenever independence and creativity persist and are productive, there is usually present an agent who plays the role of patron. Not a member of the peer group but one who possesses prestige and power in the same social setting, he could be a pastor or rabbi, or church school director. But most likely he will be the teacher. Who else has the opportunity, and who else cares so much?

12. Productive creative thinking requires fresh and new ways of looking at one's environment, at the discoveries of exploration, and at problems. The creative solution of a problem involves more than trial and error. Experiments show that it often requires a fresh insight based upon sudden shift in the way the problem is viewed. Creative thinking is not accidental success or the mere application of bits of past experience. Most problems have a structure of their own that points the way to solution, but the insight needed is often blocked or thwarted because a person clings misguidedly to some false premise or assumption of "the way it has always been done." More often than not, some fixation interferes with the use of a familiar object or idea in a novel way.

It is imperative, therefore, to see old things with new eyes. Each issue of *Highlights for Children* contains a picture in which are hidden a number of familiar objects combined with the drawing. A caption underneath the picture states, "Children of three may see these objects before adults of thirty or sixty." Why? Adults have preconceptions of just how they should appear. The parent or teacher who can maintain, or perhaps develop, the clarity and freshness of a child's perception will do much to release the creative potential of that child.

13. In addition to the foregoing suggestions for releasing and developing creative talent in children, there are several hindering attitudes which the teacher himself must overcome if he is to help his children creatively. Chief among these personal obstacles are the following:

a) Former experiences and preparation, a personal desire to conform to existing patterns in a given situation, or the insecurity of trying something different.

b) Limited success or perhaps failure in using a similar approach in the past. Failure may have been due to lack of time, overprotectiveness, lack of adequate materials, or children whose previous experience with creative approaches was so limited that they were not able to respond quickly.

c) The misconception that creativity belongs only to the arts, such as music, painting, drama, or writing.

d) Anxiety that the children will get out of hand and that discipline will be a major problem. This may be due to a misconception of what constitutes order and quiet in a classroom.

e) Limited creative success in early childhood, or being laughed at and ridiculed by adult or peer.

f) Fear of children. Fear may prevent procedures that share leadership or lessen control. A teacher may be afraid of new ideas, exploratory experiences, or children's exuberance.

g) Personal qualities such as lack of imagination, boredom, or laziness.

h) Too much "I" and not enough "we" in the attitude of the teacher. Some adults have so much or so little ego they dare not praise the success of others. When they should be supportive, they need supporting.

i) The quest for quick results. Creative teaching cannot always be measured by what one can observe quickly. It takes time.

j) Unwillingness to accept failure. In any sequence of teaching activities, some failure is likely to occur. Not every project will work, and not every child will respond. Children also need to learn about and accept failure.

k) Unwillingness to take chances. Risk-taking is a part of creating.

l) Feeling that verbal skills and common understandings are far more valuable than creative, social, or physical skills. Development of creative talent involves a wide variety of expressional forms, of which reading and writing are only two.

m) Too much emphasis upon the brightest and most gifted. The common assumption that these children alone are creative may be a block not only to creativity but also to general learning.

n) Stereotyped ideas about creative children. Not infrequently these serve as obstructions to creative development and creative teaching. How often we picture a musician with long hair, or an artist with a beard, or psychologists living with white rats, or a hermit living in a cave. Or the notion persists that creative people are at least quite neurotic if not insane.

Methods

A very extensive category of teaching methods and materials has been developed for use in the public school classroom for gifted children. It would be foolish to suggest that all of these could be used in the average religious education situation. The single most limiting factor is that of time.

For small children most church and synagogue schools could increase interest and stimulate creativity by more use of individual initiative and exploration. Use creative media, interest centers, projects, and activities that are not highly structured and preconceived, where the child's own ideas and interests can take form. Many of the prepared materials commonly used require little imagination and creativity. Far better for the gifted would be blank sheets of paper, construction materials, colors, and simple tools with merely a suggestion about what the child might do with them. Lines to be followed and well-defined spaces to be filled in are excellent materials for slow learners and retarded children, but such projects scarcely excite the gifted or even the average child.

Because of the time factor and other limitations of the usual religious education situation, one of the best methods is discussion. It has much to recommend it—no special equipment is needed, it appeals to the gifted child's excellent verbal abilities and his enjoyment of thinking and reasoning, and it allows divergent and creative thinking. Moreover, ideas, attitudes, and understandings learned through discussion are learned better and remembered longer. One word of caution: discussion should not be confused with recitation or mere answering of questions put by the teacher; it is a give-and-take, a sharing of ideas and opinions among the students as well as with the teacher.

The following incidents, observed in several of the rare religion classes that are attempting to help gifted children, are not presented as ideals or precedents to be followed or as types of learning situations limited to gifted children. They merely suggest what can be done to stimulate thinking and discussion. We share them in the hope that they will illustrate beginnings rather than ends in creative religious education.

The teacher of a class of junior high students had spent his vacation touring and camping in the West. One of the sights that had profoundly impressed him was Dinosaur National Monument, and he took a number of pictures with his 35 mm camera. He planned to use them in his class in their consideration of the Scriptural account of beginnings.

He began his lesson on Noah and the flood by reading the account from a contemporary version of the story, and then he showed his pictures of dinosaur skeletons imbedded in stone estimated conservatively at more than twenty million years old.

His beginning question: "Well, what do you think?"

Allen was quick to comment, "I thought that Noah took two of every kind of animal in his ark. How did these guys get buried? If they were some of the extra ones, what happened to those who were saved?"

"Dinosaurs were too big to put into the ark."

"The Flood story is just a story; it never really happened."

"But this book said it happened."

"I saw a program on television the other evening, and they said that most ancient civilizations had a story similar to the Flood story, so something like it must have happened."

"If only Noah's family was rescued by the ark, what I'd like to know is how the Incas of South America were saved."

"Yeah, and how did Noah get two of everything from all the other continents and islands?"

"Maybe they got there after the Flood."

"I don't see how God could be so mean to drown everyone and everything except those few in the ark. Even if the people were all bad, the animals didn't sin, did they?"

During this discussion the teacher acted as a guide and monitor to see that everyone had an opportunity to express himself. Only at the close did he offer an opinion: "I think you can see the difficulties we get into when we attempt a literal interpretation of these stories. What we must always keep in mind is that they are not from a book of science and paleontology. They were not written by geologists. What these ancient writers tell is colored by their conception of the world and the universe. This is their explanation of what they believed happened. We must remember that they were responsible only for what they knew, as we are responsible for what we know. Since we have discovered so much more truth since then, we have a far greater responsibility. What I want you to remember most of all is this: We must respect truth wherever we find it.

"Now, during this week I want you talk to everyone you can about our lesson this morning, read anything you can find on the subject—your teacher and librarian can help you—and next time we'll talk some more about Noah."

In a class of young adults, this dialogue took place:

"Do you really believe that there is life after this life?"

"What difference does it make? I couldn't care less."

"That's an awful statement to make! If you don't believe in heaven or hell, what's the use of religion?"

"If I thought that there were no life after this life, boy, I'd sure have me a ball. I'd hang being good, and I'd get me whatever I could. If you do not believe in a hereafter, what's the point of behaving yourself?"

"I believe that our belief's outstanding contribution to people today is a message of hope; life can become better. It presents some ideals for us to shoot at, and if we come anywhere near the mark, we will have achieved some measure of greater purpose and happiness."

"I get so fed up with the realism you find today in so many books, movies, and on TV. The plots can all be summed up simply: You are born in the gutter, you writhe in the gutter, you die in the gutter, and it makes no difference whether it is a gold-plated gutter or not. Where are the ideals men used to strive for? And attain in some measure, or at least they died trying. We no longer have heroes. Perhaps some of our westerns approach the hero figure, and maybe that explains their popularity. But even there, particularly in adult westerns, the main character usually has some personality quirk that finally destroys him. The tragedy is that he never even tries to overcome it. The inference is that he can't help it. Is life really so hopeless?"

"If I thought that my life would never get any better, or that I had no hope for progress, I'd take an overdose of sleeping pills right now."

"Even some brands of religion teach that man is innately depraved and has no hope for this life. He must wait for heaven —if he makes it—for anything better."

"I can't accept that. I believe that heaven or hell is 'within you' and begins here in this life. More, I believe that any man can choose which it will be. I may not be able to do everything I should, but what I can do will make my life better tomorrow than it is today."

In these classes you will note: 1) The teacher acts as a stimulator and a guide rather than an authority figure who has all the answers. 2) The children are free to ask questions and present ideas, however unusual or disturbing they may be. 3) Disagreement with traditional dogma or doctrine is not taboo or censored, but accepted. 4) Some general and helpful conclusions are suggested rather than dictated. 5) Further investigation is suggested in many instances.

Additional Qualifications for Teachers

When we make a list of the qualifications for teachers, we usually start with the sweet statement that a good teacher loves children. He does. But more than that usually implies, he has a real desire to know as much as he can about these persons, and he makes use of his knowledge as he studies with them. He also is genuinely interested in teaching them as well as he can. He is patient, sympathetic, and understanding of their complex personality. He is able to recognize and accept children as individuals in every sense of that individuality. This is a more valuable asset than a narrow enthusiasm for gifted children, which may disguise a destructive personal snobbishness which could be projected in teaching.

The teacher of gifted children should be himself interested in learning and investigation with a creative bent. If he is not hemmed in by ordinary methods, he can develop original methods and approaches and lead his students to do so. He will appreciate the creativity of his pupils. Originality, unusual ideas, and ingenuity will not be stifled. The inflexible person who thinks only in stereotypes and platitudes, who adheres to the "tried and true," has no business teaching gifted children. The teacher needs a genuinely creative approach to his subject and his method.

The teacher of a religious education class doubtless possesses certain areas of specialized knowledge and interest essential to his vocation or profession, but he must have a broad general background upon which to draw if he is to be of any real help to his pupils. He should have diversified interests which he continues to develop and which might include art, music, sports, hobbies, and drama. Any teacher should be well informed on current events. Learning is a dynamic thing that never stops.

Fairness and impartiality as well as kindliness and personal consideration are desirable traits in any teacher, but they become increasingly important in the teachers of religion for gifted children. The Judeo-Christian faiths claim to possess these qualities to a marked degree, and gifted children are unusually sensitive to their lack.

Having a highly developed sense of humor themselves, gifted children appreciate a sense of humor in their teachers. Religion often is made such a solemn and serious matter that it defeats its purpose. Fun and humor will add to, not detract from, any consideration of religion. One child put it this way: "She puts some fun into each class period, so that the whole thing seems more enjoyable. She says a class period is lost without a joke." Of course, extremes in any direction are undesirable.

The teacher who loses his temper and erects a barrier between himself and his class destroys whatever influence he may have had. The wall is not easily removed. Gifted children place a high value on self-control. A highly respected teacher was described by a talented boy: "She doesn't yell, holler, scream, shout, get angry, mad, furious, fly off the handle, pound the desk, fuss, fly into a rage, or bite your head off." Not at all? Well, maybe a little.

Psychological maturity and emotional stability are required characteristics of the good teacher. In order to accept others, he must have accepted himself. There must be self-assurance and a basic feeling of security in order to help others feel assured and secure. Maturity of emotions will stifle any jealousy of the unusual ability of the students; such feelings, obviously displayed or repressed, have no place in any classroom. In addition, a well-developed sense of personal acceptance will prevent undue sensitivity to censure and criticism.

Anyone who attempts to teach gifted children should have a better-than-average command of the subject he teaches. In the teaching of religion this would mean a thorough knowledge of the Scriptures and comprehensive understanding of the doctrines of his particular group. Some knowledge of contemporary and general theology would be valuable, as well as familiarity with other religions.

As a summary we have adapted to the teaching of religion the creed of a group of teachers at the University of North Carolina: 1) We believe that there are many gifted and talented children in our group. 2) We believe that gifted children will grow spiritually and socially where a creative program of religious education is provided for them at home and in the religious setting. 3) We believe that such an enriched program will benefit not only gifted children—but all children, the whole congregation, and the country. 4) We believe that the gifted child needs affection, understanding, security, acceptance, and the opportunity to find a personal and creative faith. 5) We believe that the gifted child should be recognized early in life, and that the religious institution should make some objective effort to identify gifted children as early as possible.

6) We believe that when special aptitudes and talents are recognized in gifted children, special provision and opportunity should be provided for their expression and development. 7) We believe that teachers should be alert to the many worthwhile channels through which all children, and especially gifted children, can be led to reasonable and creative experiences in religion. 8) We believe that the home, the congregation, and the community must work together to encourage the fullest possible religious growth of the gifted child. 9) We believe that teachers of religion to gifted children should seek every possible way to gain increasing competence in their teaching.

10) We believe that our creed is a workable philosophy when (a) there are relatively small classes, (b) when groupings or programs are based on special interests and abilities, (c) when a large variety of materials and methods are available and used, (d) when there is excellent rapport between pupils and teachers, and (e) when the work is planned in large units involving the whole religious education program over a long period of time.

The teaching of religion to gifted children may appear to be an exacting business—it is.

A Checklist for Teachers

A good teacher:

(In approximate order of importance for first 10)

1. Apparently likes his students

2. Creates a warm, relaxed, informal learning atmosphere
3. Respects the students
4. Is fair and understanding
5. Does not use sarcasm or sharp criticism
6. Welcomes questions
7. Encourages divergent viewpoints
8. Encourages student initiative
9. Really enjoys teaching and is enthusiastic
10. Works with individuals
11. Is willing to help pupils outside of class
12. Has a sense of humor
13. States objectives clearly early in class
14. Indicates clearly when moving from one major point to another
15. Causes students to think
16. Gives explanations which are clear and to the point
17. Has supporting (resource) materials which are pertinent and to the point
18. Plans lessons which provide for needs and interests and are at the experience level of pupils
19. Clarifies points with examples and illustrations
20. Uses instructions that are realistic and practical
21. Is challenging
22. Uses voice, gestures, and eyes in teaching
23. Effectively guides student ideas and activities
24. Concludes lessons with good summary of main points
25. Uses a variety of teaching methods
26. Has subject matter well-organized

8

MORAL AND SPIRITUAL VALUES
FOR GIFTED CHILDREN

M ost people share the conviction that moral and spiritual values should be taught in home, church, and school. Beyond this agreement, however, there are important questions. What is the source of moral and spiritual values? How are you to teach them? What sanctions will you use?

These questions become all the more insistent when one remembers the popular assumption that if the traditional supernatural, external, and authoritarian sources and sanctions of religion are removed from values, there is nothing left. This pessimistic assumption is based upon the false premise of the "trait" approach to character training: that these virtues reside only in either religion (God, Bible, church) or adult experience—or both—and that only religious or adult authority can enforce their application. The pupil is confronted with something foreign and external to his own experience, something imported from an eternal and authoritarian source. The problem then becomes how to impress these "traits" and virtues upon the blind and passive, and often resistant, mind of the child.

This configuration demands an authoritative approach to teaching which assumes that moral and spiritual values are not intrinsically present, actually or potentially, in all life and learning situations, but must be imported into the life or mind of the child from external source. However, as Dr. Bower says:

On the other hand, in the light of the nature of experience and of the functional relation of values to experience, as understood by the biological, psychological, and social sciences, moral and spiritual values are indigenous to the relations and functions of the school itself. More than that, if moral and spiritual values are to be real and vital and compelling in the life of the pupil, they must grow out of these relations and function in them as intrinsic motivation and control.

It cannot be otherwise when the moral and spiritual are thought of, as they should be, as qualities of the responses which pupils make to actual life situations. A response is moral when it is made to a situation through a choice of possible outcomes in the light of the growing ethical insights of mankind through generations regarding what is good and in the light of the personal and social demands of the situation itself. It is amoral when it is made without reference to these standards. It is immoral when it is made in violation of these standards.

Similarly, a response is spiritual when it is made in the widest perspectives of the world of reality, and at the highest level of the capacities of the human spirit. In the light of the earlier discussion regarding the character of the natural world, the spiritual cannot be set off in radical contrast with the physical, neither can it be identified with the "supernatural."

It is awareness of and sensitivity to the creative processes at work in nature, society, and the universe in the realm of values, which in its totality has been associated by mankind the world over with the concept of God. Moreover, spirituality carries with it the idea of devotion to that which is felt to be supremely worthful.[5]

Moral and spiritual education, then, consists of helping pupils to experience values by making moral and spiritual choices found in every situation and by carrying through their decision from intention to action. By their choices and action in concrete situations, generalized attitudes are built up into dependable patterns of behavior. The values become inner-directed, as it were, "written upon the heart."

Potential moral and spiritual values are found in every response to all social relationships and activities whenever a moral choice is involved. What happens then depends upon the awareness and sensitivity of the child, parents, or teacher to the values

[5] William Bower, *Moral and Spiritual Values in Education* (Lexington: University of Kentucky Press, 1952), pp. 76-77.

present, and to the skill used to help the child make them real and creative.

There is no easy formula which we can use to discover moral and spiritual values. More than anything else, their discovery depends upon the sensitivity of teacher and child who develop the habit of looking for them. They abound in life.

Once found, however, they should be identified and named. Otherwise, they remain vague generalities or unmanageable ideals. Spiritual values must be communicated and expressed. They thus become functional experiences valued by conscious discriminating use in reflective, purposive activities.

How to Teach These Values to Gifted Children

Before we can teach values, we must have a concept of values to serve as a guide to goals and objectives. Before a belief, attitude, or interest can be considered a value, it must meet the following criteria: [6]

1. *Values must be prized and cherished.* We may have a belief or an attitude and even act upon it, but if we wish it were different or wish it did not affect us, it cannot be considered a value.

2. *Values must involve choice after deliberation.* This frequently involves anticipation of consequences and a reflection upon the desirability of a choice. Rather than act impulsively or instinctively, we weigh, judge, and choose.

3. *Values must involve a recurring choice and action.* To make a valued judgment once and to act upon it once hardly indicates that a belief or attitude has the status of a value. Values devolve into trends and a style of life. They indicate a definite emphasis in choices and actions which tend to be repetitive.

4. *Values must affect our whole life.* If our beliefs and interests are indeed values, we will organize our life around

[6] For many ideas that follow, I am indebted to Louis E. Raths, "Clarifying Values." *Curriculum for Todays Boys and Girls,* Robert S. Fleming, Editor. (Columbus: C. E. Merrill, 1963), pp. 320-334. Used by permission of the publisher.

them. We will allot portions of time and money to support what is valued. We may develop friends, activities, hobbies, and skills consistent with what we value.

5. *Values must be something we affirm.* When challenged to stand up for our values, we know what they are for and what we are for. We demonstrate the moral courage our values represent.

Please keep in mind that it takes all five criteria to determine a value. On this basis, it must be assumed that most people have few values. As has been implied, if not stated, earlier in our discussion of values, it has become very difficult to develop values. For instance, attitudes are often mistaken for values. Sometimes we think of beliefs, purposes, aspirations, or even certain activities as values. These may become values, or a part of values, only when they meet all five criteria.

In teaching values, the basic consideration is to use methods and materials which provide opportunities for children to express attitudes, feelings, purposes, beliefs, aspirations, and interests. This expression should occur at home, in school, in the community, and in synagogue and church. As it happens, the teacher attempts to clarify the attitude or interest, and to find out if the child prizes and cherishes the attitude, or belief, or interest. He should follow up by asking the pupil:

1. about other alternative choices or activities
2. how often it comes up
3. whether he is doing anything about it in his life
4. if he needs any help to get it into his life's functioning
5. to verbalize and sum up his views
6. to affirm or deny or reject what seems to be a value

When children are asked to do these things, they often restate what they said earlier and modify it to express more clearly what they meant. Too, they rethink and examine their choices, attitudes, and actions, thus clarifying their values.

Sometimes we can help a child by asking him to tell us more about what he said. We may say that we don't see how it will work, or what the consequence will be. Or we may ask whether he believes that everyone should accept his idea, and why.

On other occasions we may examine his assumption, especially if we see some inconsistency in his reasoning or choices. At other times, he may present his idea to the class, or put it down in writing.

All of this implies that we listen carefully to what the child says. This is not easy. Parents and teachers in both public school and religious school often close their ears or listen with but one ear. A good teacher not only asks intelligent and stimulating questions; he also listens carefully. Then in addition he will react in ways to help the child develop or modify his values.

All of the above implies that we are able to get the pupil involved in expressing attitudes, beliefs, interests, feelings, purposes, and aspirations. How can we do this?

1. List many of the more important moral, social, and religious conflicts in our culture, and ask him to choose one or more to explore and evaluate carefully. Have other children do the same and have reports, round-table discussions, or debates so that there will be interactions expressing agreement, disagreement, doubt, conflicts, and conclusions.
2. Utilize world conflict situations.
3. Controversial or related issues should not be neglected or sidestepped. If the issue is a touchy one, both sides can be carefully presented. Let the child form his own conclusions.
4. Have the children write or talk about topics such as these: their attitudes toward freedom for children, religious institutions, community, home and school responsibilities; responsibilities for others less fortunate than they; allowances and earning money; using the family car and staying out late.

In all of this there are two concepts to keep clearly in mind. First, we never carry on an extended discussion with a pupil in a classroom situation. One, two or three questions, at the most involving two or three minutes, with any one child should be enough at any one time. Secondly, never argue with a student about what he says, nor reject it. Acknowledge it with some affirmative assertions to the effect that now we understand him better, or see his point more clearly. If he avoids the issue or refuses to answer a further question, drop it or talk to him at a more discreet time.

There is no way to separate value development from the thinking process. All value-type curriculum and methods will have a problem-centered character, since they invariably involve choices. They present a situation in which thinking takes place. To aid in development of values through thinking critically and creatively, we suggest the following types of activities which are adaptable to all age levels:

1. *Observing.* If children are encouraged to do purposefully what they normally do very well—look at and observe the world about them—and then are asked to evaluate orally or in writing what they saw, they develop organization, discrimination, and emphasis. As they do this, value judgments are made. Values grow out of value judgments.

2. *Classifying.* To make one's own categories is a rather high level assignment, but it is well within the abilities of gifted children. They can make lists classifying characters of the Scriptures, famous personalities of history or contemporary times, social problems, world problems, books, or words—to mention a few possibilities. The children may suggest lists, again making value judgments.

3. *Comparing.* When students are put in the position where two or more things must be contrasted and compared, where they must look for similarities and differences, thought processes are involved and value judgments are made. The list of objects, situations, problems, characters, countries, religious books, ideas, or art forms that can be used in this process is endless. However, their comparative consideration involves sensitivity, discrimination, critical thinking, and the support of these judgments. Moreover, if the student is asked to decide what similar-

ities and differences are significant, he makes a value judgment.

4. *Criticizing.* Criticism involves deep challenges to thinking. The material must be carefully examined, and points selected for criticism. The criticism in turn must be defensible, and arguments against it must be anticipated. Suitable topics for critical thinking are advertisements, TV commercials, TV programs, comic strips, and political speeches. Again the list is potentially endless. Discourage firmly the criticism of personalities, because it can hurt innocent people, develop harmful values, and impute motives no one can adequately examine.

5. *Analyzing.* Most concepts, institutions, arts, materials, productions, stories, propaganda—to name a few things—can be analyzed by students in gifted groups if they are given a list of criteria with which to work. There are literally hundreds of applications of this function. As the students apply the sets of criteria, thought is required and value judgments made.

6. *Imagining.* This type of thinking is limited only by the imagination of the teacher. A common method is that in which a story is begun, or a situation presented, and the student is asked to complete the story, or to explain the cause of or the way out of the situation. Or we may ask them to describe their most unusual experiences, or what they would do if they had three wishes. In all of these and hundreds of others like them, the students make value judgments and choices.

7. *Planning.* This might involve planning a field trip, a vacation, a party, a paper, a money-raising project, a summer camp program, civic improvements, youth meetings, or recreation programs. Here again are opportunities to clarify and develop value judgments.

8. *Research and exploration.* The pupil is engaged in learning or investigating something he is concerned about. It can take the form of a poll or interview to find out, for instance, how peers spend their allowance, or what they do in their leisure time. It might involve an original prob-

lem. Or a trip to another town, church, synagogue, library, or museum. Laboratory equipment may be used. Whatever the problem or activity selected for investigation, there is great opportunity for thought, accumulation of knowledge, selection of knowledge, value judgments, and generalizations.

9. *Summarizing.* Summarizing is one of the best ways to develop discrimination. What will be included in the summary? What left out? Why? How will it be organized? What should be emphasized? Or not stressed? Some gifted children will attempt to avoid this activity, or will include every little detail. This experience is needed to develop critical and discriminating thinking. It results in choices, which are an essential part of value development.

Our hypothesis and objectives are simple. If children are constantly, deliberately exposed to situations in which they must think and evaluate, and if their responses are clarified and accepted, they will develop the ability to make value judgments and decisions. This is one of the most effective ways to develop a schemata of values and the self-discipline needed in value decision-making. The step between making amoral value judgments and decisions and those based upon moral and spiritual values is a very short one. Once the basic attitudes and skills are developed, it is then merely the matter of identifying the moral and spiritual values involved in making such judgments and decisions. The whole procedure is transferable.

For values of any sort to be the prized and personal set of behavior guidelines which are desired, they must not be imposed by one person upon another, either by coercion or by indoctrination. Persuasion has no place in teaching beliefs and values. This is not to say that the teacher of values may not help the child to identify and clarify the attitudes, interests, aspirations, and values involved in making a choice. A child may need to have pointed out the possible courses of action, and he may need to have their consequences clarified. But the choice should be his without coercion or intimidation. Too often we say the person is a free moral agent, but then act as if he were no such thing. He must be free to choose or not to choose, to act or not to act, to change or not to change. Values or the lack of them determine personality and character. Good character and personality develop when good values are clarified and internalized.

Examples of Teaching Moral and Spiritual Values

The following examples are given merely to illustrate one way of using incidents to clarify and teach values. They should not be considered the only way, nor should they be considered as examples of counseling in any depth. Some children have deeply seated personality and emotional problems. No unqualified person should attempt therapy; this is work for the professional counselor, psychologist, or psychiatrist. What are given here are rather simple problems effectively used to clarify values. Not all situations will be as simple, nor will they all work as effectively.

In a class of junior high pupils, Jimmy, a new boy, was constantly "finding" small change. It soon became evident to everyone that Jimmy was lying and stealing. The basic value of honesty was involved in this experience.

"Just why should we be honest?" asked the teacher.

"If you don't, you'll go to hell," replied Susan.

"Aw, I don't believe in hell," said Jimmy.

"If I didn't believe in hell, I'd never be good. I'd take whatever I wanted, and I'd hardly ever tell the truth." Susan did her best to rebuke Jimmy.

"Well, now, suppose that everyone felt as you do. What do you think would happen?"

"Not everyone would feel like that," retorted Jimmy.

"I hope not, but *suppose* they did," insisted the teacher.

"You couldn't trust anyone; they'd take whatever you had. I couldn't trust anyone, and they'd steal all my things," admitted Jimmy.

"Exactly!"

"That would be awful! I couldn't mail a letter, or order things from Sears. I couldn't ever trust my teachers or parents." The light began to dawn for Jimmy.

"Isn't that, then, a good reason for being honest yourself?"

"I guess so—yes, it is."

Jack was an excellent first baseman, but he was only a fair hitter at bat. To compensate for his lack, he would blame the umpires for unfairness in calling his strikes. The values involved were fair play and responsibility for one's own failures.

The coach had tried a number of ways to help Jack see his problem. This time he tried to help Jack see the basic values and choices involved.

"Jack, why do we have umpires?"

"I guess so we have someone to call the shots."

"Why?"

"Some guys won't play fair."

"Is that all? Can you always tell when a ball is high or inside?"

"No, I guess not."

"Suppose all the fellows always blamed the umpire for their outs? What would happen?"

"It wouldn't be fair!"

"But it's fair to you."

"That's different."

"Is it? Is he picking on you? Do you think you are different, or that he should give you more breaks than he does the others?"

"No, not really, when I think of it."

"What is the real trouble, then?"

"I guess it's because I'm not a good hitter, and I think he should give me a break to even it out."

"Don't you suppose a little more batting practice would be a better solution to your problem? I'm sure you want to be fair, and I'm sure you'd like to become a better hitter."

"You're right. I really would."

Mary was a bright but bored fourth grader. She easily memorized and verbalized all the familiar Bible verses that had to do with getting along with other children. She could recite flawlessly the Sermon on the Mount. But she was constantly teasing

the other children and causing an uproar in class. Various puni-
tive disciplinary measures were tried. She was preached to and
warned of eternal damnation, all with no success. Finally, the
teacher resigned, literally a nervous wreck. Mary needed to be
challenged and interested, but she also needed to understand the
meaning of kindness. The new teacher found the first easier
than the second.

Then one day she noticed that Mary became quite upset when
another girl teased her. After class she asked Mary to stay a
few moments.

"I noticed you crying a little this morning. Would you care
to tell me why?"

"I got mad!"

"Why?"

"Susan was kicking me under the table."

"Did it hurt?"

"Not much, but I hate to be tormented, and I wanted to
listen to you."

"Did you ever tease her?"

"Yes, I guess so."

"How do you suppose she liked it?"

"She didn't. I made her cry once."

"What do you suppose would happen if all the pupils in this
class teased everyone else as you did Susan?"

"You'd probably go nuts, and we'd never learn anything.
We'd probably need a lot of Kleenex, too."

"What is the opposite of teasing and hurting others?"

"Being kind, I guess."

"Do you like to be treated kindly?"

"Sure, I do."

"Do you suppose all the pupils feel the same way?"

"Yes, I suppose so."

"Let's try something. When you feel like teasing, why don't
you do something nice instead and see what happens?"

"Okay. I'll try. I really will."

These all have been rather extreme cases and involve teaching
values as solutions to well-developed problems. Some teaching

of moral and spiritual values will deal with this type of problem, but values can grow out of all kinds of experiences, and ideally, should prevent rather than cure character defects.

Jerry was a first grader and a newcomer in the community. He was eight and large for his age, but he had a slight limp and a noticeable speech defect as a result of polio when he was three. He was pale and shy, and forsaken-looking. He seemed to have no social talent whatever, but, worse, it quickly was apparent that he was going to become the object of ridicule by the rest of the class. The teacher then discovered that Jerry had an unusual talent for art. The class needed to learn respect for others, and Jerry needed self-respect. So she immediately began to use that talent. She praised his work before the class, showed it to his parents and other teachers, and asked him to illustrate many of the lessons. In the finger painting and creative work of the class Jerry was an able helper to the teacher. Through Jerry's unusual talent, she found a way to help the children overlook his handicap by appreciation of his ability in art. This recognition gave Jerry self-respect and security in the class.

One boy in a primary class expressed the wish never to do anything but what he wanted to. Most of the class expressed the same desire, but agreed that at the same time they should not do anything that would hurt anyone or destroy property. So the next week the teacher announced that this morning they could do just as they pleased, as long as they observed the rules made the week before. The children were delighted—at first. Soon they became bored and frustrated and wanted "something to do."

Said one girl, "I guess we need a little help in doing what we want. It's no fun doing nothing too long." It is quite likely that had sufficient materials been provided and some guidance offered, the children could also have learned to take advantage of free time in developing self-motivated work habits, taste for books, and hobbies.

These few examples illustrate how moral and spiritual values can be found in actual experiences and developed into attitudes that build character.

A List of Potential Values

Briefly, here is a list of potential values that can be found by those who develop a sensitivity to them and who look for them in life situations: (1) skill in making choices and value judgments; (2) a feeling of achievement; (3) an open-minded critical and reflective attitude toward different or new ideas; (4) respect for the rights, opinions, and beliefs of others; (5) understanding the universe as a place of law, order, and logic; (6) sympathy, kindness, and understanding of others that results in (7) a willingness to sacrifice for the welfare of others; (8) sharing of some ability, time, or material; (9) honesty in all personal relationships; (10) fair play and justice for all; (11) obedience to law; (12) respect and equality for minorities; (13) a feeling of responsibility for community and nation; (14) an understanding and respect for the worth of every person as an individual; (15) an appreciation of beauty and aesthetic values wherever they may be found; (16) respect for an appreciation of all kinds of productive labor; (17) group loyalty and co-operation; (18) understanding and appreciation of the consequences of one's acts; (19) personal integrity; (20) belief in and respect for some creative and guiding power higher than man which we commonly call God; (21) a sense of stewardship of time, ability, and material goods; and (22) a worthy purpose and reason for being.

In teaching these values, one should always keep in mind that they should not usually be sought in problem or crisis situations, but in the everyday experiences of life. They will frequently be found to be in conflict with the standards of mass society, in which case careful evaluation of their worth and social implications should be made. This is not to say that they should be abandoned if conflict arises, or revised when there is pressure to conform. Reflective evaluation will decide their intrinsic worth.

One more matter of vital importance: in teaching moral and spiritual values, more than in any other area, parents and teachers influence their children with their own behavior and attitudes. One can hardly lead children along paths that he himself has not walked.

9

CHALLENGING THE GIFTED CHILD

No MATTER how phenomenally gifted a person may be, if he lacks motivation he will accomplish nothing either in self-satisfying pursuits or in benefits to society. It is impossible even to estimate the tremendous waste of talent that is undirected and unchallenged. In a religious sense we regard abilities which are used for selfish ends, with no sense of spiritual purpose, as wasted. In public education this lack of motivation is called underachievement or lack of drive; in religion, lack of dedication or commitment.

We may describe underachievement further by saying it is achievement and interest which are below the level consistent with the abilities of a person—when the ten-talented person has buried one or nine, if not all ten, of his talents. For some reason he is not using all of his abilities. We are discovering that the ten-talented child most often lacks drive and inspiration, but anyone who does less than best with his abilities is to that degree an underachiever. It is interesting to note that boys far outnumber girls in this failure to achieve at the level of their abilities. Dr. Merle Sumption of the University of Illinois states that underachievement is the primary problem in the educational guidance of the gifted child. It is one of the major problems in religious education as well.

There are many reasons for this sad state of affairs, and the underachiever may lack motivation for one or more of them. Sometimes it is due to habits of sloth and laziness, growing out of the ability to meet standards easily and with little effort. Sometimes it is the practiced result of a wish to conform to peer standards, or to escape ridicule as a "brain" or a "grind." Poor attitudes and study habits grow out of these practices. In other cases broken or unhappy homes, poor health, or extreme poverty destroys the will to excell. (However, in some cases these same factors work paradoxically to stimulate achievement.) A major cause of underachievement in religious education is the boredom and frustration growing out of the routine of common practices, described in detail in previous chapters. In reality this is underachievement by underteaching, but its effect is nonetheless devastating.

Not infrequently gifted boys and girls are discouraged by parents who take their religion so casually as to be meaningless, or so seriously as to be fanatics. Either extreme offends the logic and sensibilities of gifted children. Demands and expectations set too high or too low are equally destructive of the will to use ability. Gifts that are neglected or penalized are often destroyed. No doubt a major cause of underdeveloped and unused abilities stems from what is sometimes called one's self-concept. Any teacher, pastor, or rabbi can tell of instances when some responsibility was refused with, "I can't do it." The excuse was given sincerely in most cases. The underachiever refuses to believe anything which would suggest that his picture of himself is false. His concept of self is so firmly entrenched that he stubbornly resists any overt attempt to show that it is unrealistically low.

Stimulating Commitment

Every teacher and many parents are familiar with the able youngster who lacks involvement or commitment. To put it another way, we say he lacks motivation. Lack of involvement and commitment results in lack of intrinsic motivation. He has not been able to, or does not seem to want to, enter into meaningful relationships at home, at school, at synagogue or church. As a result he displays little or no interest in these institutions or the ideas for which they stand. In school he may be an underachiever, at home a problem, in the religious group a disinterested bystander—bored with life in general.

Finding satisfactory involvement is essential to adequate living and successful performance in any human endeavor. To discover purpose and point is to find fulfillment in the things one is doing. No constructive action and no learning of any consequence take place without a high degree of involvement and commitment on the part of the individual.

In less prosperous times it seemed far easier to become involved. In an affluent culture the problem of finding something worth dying for, or living for, becomes a difficult question. What shall a person devote himself to in so replete a society? What shall he work for? What can he do to make a contribution?

These are hard questions for adults. They are frightening and discouraging questions for younger persons as they find themselves confronted with a culture that has conspired to prevent them from becoming involved or committed to anything. We are overproducing materialistic comforts and overprotecting them, but at the same time we are putting them under powerful pressures to learn, learn, learn. For what? Money, status, influence? These are extrinsic motivations. *The essential intrinsic motivation is missing.* Prepared better and better to do less and less, kept out of adult concerns as long as possible, they have built with the aid of merchandisers a society of their own—their own music, magazines, language, dress, code of ethics, TV programs, customs, and symbols of status and prestige. They have developed their own reasons for being because they have no other commitments.

This waste cannot long be tolerated. The loss in human potential is tremendous, the loss in human happiness even greater. We must be concerned not only because we love our young people, important as that may be, but because the very institutions we value and society itself are in danger. Those who do not feel that they really belong to an institution see no reason why they should be committed to what it stands for.

I believe that our gifted youngsters want to be committed, to be involved, to have a worthwhile purpose for living. Our homes, religious groups, and our schools have vital responsibilities in helping children find commitment. We must find ways of developing intrinsic motivation.

Caught or taught? It is often stated that religion, values, and commitment cannot be taught, but must be caught. The implication is that they are attained by accident rather than by plan. The author subscribes, however, to the belief that motivation and involvement are attitudes based upon values, and values are developed. As such they can be taught—taught by example and by design. Still, it must remain to some degree a *personal* discovery that an idea or a cause is worthwhile and fulfilling. This discovery comes out of challenge and motivation. Usually some other person is involved and involves the child; he can be a parent, a teacher, a friend, a hero.

Some Principles of Motivation

One of the most ambitious and significant studies on this subject was conducted by Morse and Wingo.[7] They asked several hundred good teachers how they motivated their students. Frequently, the teachers were at a loss to explain what they did. In general, their explanations were an oversimplification and belied the subtlety of the actual teaching skill that was observed. It is a rare teacher who has the insight and objectivity to measure validly his own teaching ability. The authors found that students were far more able to make evaluations of their teachers.

A good many teachers say they challenge students by *expecting them to work*. Schools are for learning; they never intimate that it might be otherwise. Such teachers motivate by their attitudes and methods used in making assignments, asking questions, or presenting interesting information. In their opinion, most students really like to learn. All the pupils need, they believe, is to be guided through tasks which are reasonable and clearly set by an understanding teacher who anticipates student compliance. These teachers believe, and it works for them,

[7] William C. Morse and G. Max Wingo, *Psychology and Teaching* (Chicago: Scott, Foresman and Company, 1962), pp. 288-290. Used by permission of publisher.

that when students clearly understand exactly what is expected of them and know that they have a good chance of succeeding, they will "work their heads off."

"I find something that interests him" is a frequent answer by teachers who feel that there is enough intrinsic interest in most learning tasks to motivate the average student. Almost invariably these teachers also impart a feeling that success is possible. Probably most teachers who are successful with this method underestimate the basic importance of their own security and interest in their work—as well as their ability to gauge the nature of their students, establish a secure learning atmosphere, and impart the feeling that pupils and teacher are engaged in a mutual effort toward a worthwhile achievement. The student senses that the teacher is "with" him, not against him or indifferent to him.

Other teachers do not expect school tasks to be self-motivating. They feel that there is not enough intrinsic interest in most tasks and that students must be motivated by *pressures and threat of failure* or enticed to learn by *promises of enjoyment and reward*—sometimes both. As pressure mounts, the results are not infrequently far from the ones desired: some pupils will work harder, others feel that the demands are unreasonable, and still others become rebellious and look for ways to retaliate against a system that makes them so uncomfortable. Only a few are motivated to real achievement by pressures and threats. When competition exists between a student and a teacher, cooperation and mutual encouragement are not likely to develop. A vicious circle, though, does develop—pressure and threats induce failure which produces more pressure and threats which lead to failure.

There is a difference between being challenged and being threatened. An individual feels challenged when he confronts a situation he feels he has a chance of handling adequately. He feels threatened when he confronts a demand that implies or is associated with failure or punishment. Our problem is how to help him feel challenged without feeling threatened. Unfortunately, we cannot always tell. We must understand that what is challenging or motivating is not determined by a parent or a teacher, but by the child himself.

Whatever threatens, embarrasses, or degrades a person's self-concept is not only discouraging and humiliating; it is also stultifying and stupifying. No learning can possibly take place in such a situation, and certainly no challenge to involvement and commitment. Such acts actually destroy what we can measure as intelligence; IQ scores actually go down in such an environment. Pressure put on as pressure will usually fail. Parents or teachers who nag, expect too much, or are too perfectionistic will almost always end up with an underachiever.

It is important to note, however, that pressures may be positive—if they are combined with acceptance, understanding, and a challenge which arouses curiosity and interest. This may lead to involvement as the child exerts pressures from within to do what he is able to do and now is eager to do. External pressure of any sort is of little value. Inner pressure that induces involvement is effective, and there is little danger of backfiring.

Few teachers knowingly induce pressure to the point of producing real anxiety. Yet many teachers must make their students overanxious without realizing it, as examination tension and fear of failure are all too common among students. What such fear-producing stress does to pupil-teacher relationships was demonstrated in a classic experiment by H. A. Murray. He found that when pupils were made fearful and then shown a series of pictures, they imputed more maliciousness to the adults shown in the pictures than when fear was not first induced. Teachers or parents who, knowingly or unknowingly, cultivate fear can be expected to be perceived as threatening. This response tends to broaden to a fear of school in general and a dislike of all school subjects and activities. We know, too, from other studies, that when an individual feels threatened his perceptions become more narrow, his responses less flexible, and he becomes defense-oriented rather than task-oriented. This reaction can hardly be expected to improve achievement in any setting.

Pressure has another unfortunate result. In working to meet parent or teacher demands, the learner may fail to develop any feeling of responsibility for directing his own learning or for setting up standards for himself. Instead of being self-propelled, he becomes dependent upon an outside authority to keep him task-oriented. Many studies have shown that college students who have never learned to plan or direct their own learning need frequent tests to keep them study-oriented. When such students first encounter a situation in which they learn because of their own seeking, their satisfaction is dramatically different from the feeling they had under pressured learning. When students are given the opportunity to make a change from pressured learning to self-direction, they feel lost and insecure—but not for long. The new and more pleasant satisfaction leads to a remarkable adjustment.

Many of the teachers studied by Morse and Wingo report that they try to motivate by *making the student's efforts satisfying and pleasurable.* If the pupil likes the experience, he will learn more, say these teachers. This claim is supported by considerable research. For example, it has been found that more was retained when the attitude was favorable, and that students did better in problem-solving tasks when they expected to succeed than when they did not, regardless of the difficulty of the tasks. Students motivated by pressures and fear of failure express goals below their own actual accomplishment, but those motivated by anticipation of success and rewards tend to set goals higher than their level of accomplishment. Teachers who try to make learning satisfying use a wide range of devices including teacher recognition, group acknowledgment, and parental support for work well done. Praise is their keystone, and marks are regarded as symbols of reward.

Teachers and psychologists alike have long emphasized the importance of rewards. Many experimenters have found that incentives can stimulate learning in both animal and human subjects. Rewarding a correct response seems to increase the likelihood that it will occur again. It has even been seriously proposed that a school be established where pupils would be paid cash to learn. The more one would learn, the more he would earn. This might be an interesting experiment in design, but no one expects it to become a pattern for American public or religious schools. Classroom rewards must usually be less tangible.

Even such an apparently simple motivational device as parent or teacher "praise" or "blame" is enormously complicated and may have varying effects under different conditions. Originally, it was found that praise was more effective than blame in motivating pupil effort. But since this pioneer study, it has been discovered that a number of qualifications must be added to their conclusions. For example, it makes a difference who administers the praise or blame. If the person is one held in high esteem, praise can be potent; but if the person is looked down on, blame from him may be regarded as more desirable than praise—as proof that the recipient is in the "enemy camp"! Praise given out by an unpopular teacher may thus have a negative result.

Expectations, rewards, and pressures—these, essentially, were the three answers given by teachers to the question, "How do you motivate students?" Yet they obviously used far more intricate motivational techniques than they listed.

Even though the teachers interviewed did not list interpersonal relationships as motivators, experience shows that such relationships are a prime factor. Perhaps without realizing exactly how they operate, many effective teachers depend on a personal relationship of mutual interest and confidence in which they provide emotional support and bolster the pupil's confidence in himself. Liking and admiring a teacher provides an incentive to do well and live up to his expectations. Undoubtedly, too, many effective teachers make learning satisfying by supporting the work impulses already present in their pupils, by kindling new interests, and by holding to requirements suited to the capability of their students.

For those who are concerned with challenging and motivating children who have chronically lacked involvement, recent studies by Gallagher [8] offer help. He found these methods of motivating the underachiever to be the least successful:

---

[8] James J. Gallagher, *Teaching the Gifted* (Boston: Allyn and Bacon, Inc., 1964), pp. 233-238. Used with permission.

1. The inspirational talk, or "get-in-there-and-fight-fellows" approach.
2. Personal counseling of various types when used without other approaches. (We are speaking of only the underachiever. Counseling may be very effective in dealing with other problems of the gifted.)
3. Externally applied pressures of every sort.

However, when these children were given a warm, accepting, flexible, and challenging teacher, they responded with higher achievement. When, in addition, they were grouped in classes or clubs with other children of similar ability, achievement and commitment notably improved.

Most attempts to motivate chronic underachievers have failed. But this study by Gallagher (and others since then) indicates that it is possible to improve motivation and learning by modifying attitudes. This can be accomplished not by attacking poor motivation directly, but rather through a modification of the educational environment. In these experimental classes the underachievers were introduced to a warmer, more accepting, and more stimulating environment than they had experienced before. External pressures, threats, and fear of failure were removed. Presented with an attainable challenge, they responded. These studies indicate beyond question that the single most important factor in motivation is the teacher (or parent) who provides warmth, affection, understanding, and acceptance.

Methods of Motivation

There are no simple or easy formulas or infallible methods by which we can secure adequate motivation. Nor is there such a thing as a typical case. Every situation is different and must be handled differently. In some rare cases lack of motivation seems to cure itself when the child becomes caught by an absorbing interest. Sometimes a parent or teacher is able to provoke interest sufficient to motivate a reluctant child. Intensive counseling works in only a few instances. But in far too many cases, the disease seems incurable.

As in the case in all pathological maladies, prevention works far better than cure. It is primarily to this end that the following suggestions are offered. Even occasional success is cause of great rejoicing.

1. Use modern methods and techniques of education in the home and in religious classes. As Gallagher's studies found, good teaching is the single most important source of adequate motivation and inspiration.

2. Build upon an established interest. The case of a boy to whom the writer once taught geometry illustrates this principle. The implications are equally valid for secular and religious education.

   John was one of the most highly gifted children I ever taught, and he was at the same time one of the greatest underachievers, in all his studies. Soon after school began, John wanted to drop geometry because he "couldn't do it." The principal and I persuaded him to stay in the class. I soon noticed that he paid little attention to what went on and instead was usually reading *Popular Science* or *Popular Mechanics*. One day without saying anything to him, I began to make drawings on the board, applying geometrical principles to mechanics. I noticed that Johnny had stopped reading and was listening. After the class he stayed a few moments to ask whether I would tell him some more about geometry and mechanics. Of course I would. It seems unreasonable to say that his attitude toward geometry changed overnight, but it did. He stayed after school, spent study periods in an empty classroom working on advanced geometry problems. In the spring he placed second in the Ohio State Achievement Tests in plane geometry. This is not all—he became a top student in his other classes and was class president in his senior year and editor of the annual. This is an unusual case of interest used to cure underachievement. It does not always succeed so easily, but it is worth a good try.

   Luckily most bright and gifted children do have special interests, and usually they are easily discovered. The problem is to make effective use of them for solving the problem at hand. It should not be an arbitrary or artificial relationship, for the gifted child will probably see through the subterfuge. Nevertheless, imagination and awareness can often find a way to use an interest to capture interest. However, it is possible to overdo a good thing until the child and the class are tired of it. Besides, interests do not always remain fixed. Our goal is to discover and develop new interests.

To challenge a child by means of his interest, (1) talk to him about it and show an interest in his learning; (2) show him how he can increase both the breadth and depth of it—there is virtually no limit to this; (3) assign a report on the hobby; (4) set up a project that uses it, and let him lead it; (5) arrange hobby shows and exhibitions as rewards; (6) sometimes give him the responsibility of helping another pupil who lacks his ability or skill.

3. Encourage identification. A primary means is by relationships with persons he can admire and respect. Social imitation which arises from personal involvement with others is a strong motivator. All children learn from other people's behavior. They gain some estimate of their own values as they evaluate others. This is especially important in character development and in religious attitudes. One way to test how effectively this learning is taking place is to observe the child's use of the cooperative pronouns *we, our,* and *us.* They signify identification. The use of *I* and *mine, you* and *yours* or *they* and *theirs* to the exclusion of the cooperative terms indicates a lack of identification, and, if excessive, rebellion.

Nothing is more destructive to identification with a person or with what he believes than inconsistency between theory and practice. Sincerity and honesty, even with low performance, are to be desired above hypocrisy and insincerity.

Inspiration by identification need not always be first-hand. It can be vicarious, an almost unlimited experience. A character on the television or movie screen or from a book may appeal to the child as someone to emulate. Especially valuable are biographies. Many a person has been challenged and motivated by the life of a man or woman who became real in the pages of a book.

Obviously, the effect of vicarious identification can have a reverse effect as well. It is therefore important that what a child sees or reads be carefully chosen, which is no limitation. There is a wealth of excellent material for one who cares enough to choose the best.

4. Competition is sometimes suggested as an excellent means of motivation. It is highly overrated. For those who always win, it may be effective; but for the many who are bound to lose, the result is discouraging. Competition is probably at its best when a child competes with himself, but even here goals must be realistic and within range of achievement.

In recent years there has been a trend to recommend competition especially for gifted children. Those who do so maintain that children must be prepared to live in a competitive society by learning how to excel. Even if it succeeds as a motivator, the unfortunate side effects far outweigh any benefits. It emphasizes personal prestige and aggrandizement based on achievement over others. It tends to produce the attitude that progress can only be made by surpassing someone else—which is false on the face of it and from a religious viewpoint unacceptable.

Competition neglects the fact that much success depends upon cooperation and interdependence. Not all children make progress by competing. Some are too fearful, and many do not need to compete to find a challenge. Some children neglect important activities or engage in less useful pursuits in order to win a prize, be chosen valedictorian, or make the honor roll. Popular aspects of approval tend to outweigh the more essential. Science exhibits tend to replace science itself, for instance. Self-criticism, social responsibility, initiative, and creativity often suffer from prize-getting competition. Creativity more often than not is stifled rather than promoted by competition, for it involves risk and may not succeed.

In competitive situations failure is an eminent, constant threat. The child cannot afford to try the unusual, but will tend to do that which is known to be correct and acceptable. Research and experimentation rarely thrive on competition, and complex or highly imaginative procedures are the first to be eliminated through the sheer necessity of winning on time.

Furthermore, the deceptively destructive element of competition often causes losers to withdraw from the activities it is supposed to develop. The image of failure is reinforced; fear and distrust or aggression and hostility may be promoted. Extremely damaging are the false standards of value set up. The prize becomes the symbol of success and victory, and prizes (and praise and grades) are artificial motivations. Gifted children above all others are most likely to see through the artifice.

A characteristic of gifted children is the ability to postpone satisfactions. Competition sets immediate goals and rewards, and in its usual forms does nothing to strengthen postponement of satisfactions or develop long-range goals.

Forgotten are the values of service and sacrifice. Moral virtues and spiritual values can hardly be motivated by competition without injecting the evil of pride. It is hardly an achievement worth the effort.

All of this is not to say that competition has no place as a motivating factor. It cannot be eliminated from life. But it should be used sparingly and wisely in teaching religion and spiritual values. When it is used, children need to understand that neither losing nor winning is necessarily permanent in the life situation—though they may appear to be so from many competitively motivated learning situations. When parents and teachers are aware of the dangers involved, many of them may be minimized if not avoided.

5. Recognition may be profitably used. While its rewards seem closely related to the prizes of competition, there is a vital difference between the two. The second seeks laurels by winning over others, while the first seeks reward for effort and achievement in one's own right.

The desire for recognition and appreciation can be satisfied in many ways. The young child seeks approval and attention from his parents, and finds security in it. When he grows older, he wants value recognition for what he does. If this recognition does not come, he will compel attention in other ways such as misbehaving, talking too much, or not working. One of the best arguments for grouping bright children together is that intellectual achievement will be more readily recognized and honored. Acceleration is another reward.

Rewards of all kinds work best with those whose achievements are high, but do not usually serve as a challenge to underachievers. The reward of recognition is, however, at its best used as a preventive. If good work and good behavior are recognized as honorable from early childhood, more children will do their best from the beginning.

6. Be sparing with that which is novel and unique. Many teachers constantly seek some new method of presentation or strange idea with which to interest their pupils. Some variation and novelty do help to keep interest, but when used primarily for the sake of being different they may even be harmful. Constant change and variety may increase insecurity and dependence rather than creativity.

Children find freedom and security from the familiar. When an experience is so new and the challenge so great that feelings of insecurity are aroused, the possibility for learning and growth is inhibited. The overpowering need for self-preservation may cause intelligent reaction to be replaced by random panic responses.

This is true not only when too many strange factors are introduced into a learning situation, but also when the assigned tasks are too far above what a child is able to achieve. Unless variety and challenge are introduced slowly and carefully, they may cause dependence and destruction of personality.

7. Curiosity is a powerful motive in the gifted. When there is also an opportunity to investigate by handling and manipulating some unusual object or puzzle, the challenge becomes even greater. This introduces a factor of controlling the situation and reduces feelings of insecurity.

Some successful teachers begin their class period by placing a strange object where it can be easily seen and handled. Children are encouraged to bring items of their own. All persons like to solve riddles and work puzzles, and learning activities with an incomplete element or puzzling quality are interesting. When directions are too clear and easily followed or the work too easily completed, interest is lost.

When a student sets out to find how and why something works, or why it is true or false, there is literally no end to the amount of effort he will exert. Children need something to get their hands and minds on—something not easy to solve, but not impossible either.

Curiosity is easy to stimulate, but also easy to smother. Meaningless detail seldom fails. For instance, memorizing meaningless Scripture passages in relation to some project, however interesting, will kill both. Whatever is done must have real significance. When a parent or teacher hears an interested "Why?" or "How?" he can be sure he has stirred the powerful force of curiosity. Let him be sure that he does not kill it off by denying its expression. In religious matters it is especially easy to imply, "You must not touch! This is too sacred to examine!"

8. The spiritual and social values of a family are strong motivators which are not easily manipulated. Family background is important. Lewis Terman, one of the pioneers in the study of gifted children, says, "No other factor so strikingly differentiates" their success.

The factors of education, achievement, vocation, reading, self-improvement, expectation, artistic interests, religion, and social standing have a direct effect on the aspirations and goals of gifted children in direct proportion to their level. Of course, there are exceptions. Unusually high expectations defeat and discourage gifted children, and too much blame and criticism create anxiety which becomes a life-long hindrance.

Several recent studies indicate that the higher the intelligence, the more inappropriate and destructive are punishment and criticism. In adults punishment may merely inhibit a response, but in a child it may develop a long-lasting anxiety that may invade other activities and interfere with motivation. Some tension and anxiety are characteristic of intelligence, but intense anxiety is destructive.

Constructive criticism which sees error and points to a better response can be helpful. Too much criticism shouts, "Stop! You are wrong!" Self-criticism in gifted children is characteristic, and their self-evaluation encourages growth and development in all areas. Added criticism by parents or teachers may be just too much.

But one factor is decisive in making the home conducive either to high dedication and achievement or to poor motivation and low accomplishment—it is the pervasive atmosphere. Unfortunately, it is not easily improved. For the most part the home either has what it takes to inspire gifted children or it does not. It is possible for a good atmosphere to become better, and sometimes the church or synagogue miraculously compensates for what a home may lack. However, most of the inspirational forces and attitudes are usually present or not present in the home when the child is born.

9. Purpose always accompanies high achievement and dedication. Any worthwhile accomplishment needs a reason or a cause which the performer perceives as worthwhile. This purpose must be more than an immediate satisfaction. The individual must be able to fix upon a distant goal, plan how to reach it, and persist in his efforts to achieve it.

The innate characteristics of the gifted include both the intense desire for a purpose and the ability to plan ahead and work for the distant goals. The problem is to find a purpose or a goal that is challenging and which seems attainable.

Gordon Allport writes in his book *Becoming,* "The possession of long-range goals, regarded as central to one's personal existence, distinguishes the human being from the animal, the adult from the child, and in many cases the healthy personality from the sick." If you can help a child learn how to plan ahead and work for future satisfactions, or do one thing to be able to do another, you build a sense of purpose. As he grows older, he can be helped to look farther ahead. Nurture an ambition or set a goal which captures his imagination and interest, and motivation and inspiration will come readily.

Harry Emerson Fosdick, in his book *The Power To See It Through* says, ". . . staying power is always associated with the experience of being captured by a cause, laid hold on by something greater than oneself to which one gives one's loyalty—an art, a science, a vocation, a social reform, an object of devotion which one conceives to be more important than oneself." This is the motivating force that always accompanies the persistent character of men like Lincoln, Jonas Salk, and Albert Schweitzer. All of these men found a cause to which they gave their loyalty in spite of persecution, fortune, or sacrifice. All persistent long-range goals are associated with such purpose.

To have one major purpose is indeed essential, but

there ought to be other lesser purposes, and they need not be directly related to the larger goal. Achievement is no great leap from hither to yon, but a series of steps each leading to the next. They should be recognizable as steps, although each may be fairly complete in itself.

When a child begins to sense a purpose, nurture and encourage it carefully. Attention, praise, guidance, opportunities for more knowledge about it, and expression or use of some part of it will do wonders to fan the spark. Suppose he changes his mind later on? Or suppose what he chooses now is not a worthy goal? These questions are often asked about children who begin to look ahead. Don't worry; changes do no harm. There is virtue in direction and effort to achieve a goal, whatever it is. The sad cases are those with no direction or purpose whatever.

Some children, however, who are going along seemingly goal-less, suddenly find themselves and a purpose. They see where they want to go. They are captured by a cause, apparently by chance. Perhaps they were stimulated by a teacher, a friend, a new hobby, a book, a course in school—and this is it. This is the time parents, teachers, and clergymen hope and pray for, particularly for those who may have been underachievers.

10. A major and final source of motivation is a sense of stewardship. This concept is founded on the basis that one's gifts are just that, gifts from God. They have been entrusted to one's care to be developed and used to their fullest capacity in the expression of one's personality, in service to mankind, and to the glory of the Giver. To teach this concept diligently and carefully is a privilege and an opportunity. The person with great talent is blessed. When that talent is used for a worthy purpose, he is twice blessed.

Gifted children have a right, perhaps even an obligation, to know who they are and what they can do in life. What are appropriate goals? To what extent should they think of themselves as leaders? Innovators and creative thinkers? What are their responsibilities?

Two close friends, Frank and Bob, who were moderately gifted were working only enough to get by so that they would be eligible to play football. There was a third boy, Steve, who had to work hours to accomplish what they could do in minutes so that he, too, would be eligible. One day I asked Frank and Bob to see me after lunch. "Have you fellows ever thought of how fortunate you are?"

"Why? How?" They were obviously puzzled, but interested by my question.

"Have you ever noticed how hard Steve has to work to stay on the team?" They had.

"Do you know why he must work so much longer than you, fellows?" They were not sure, but they guessed he just learned more slowly than they did.

"That's true. You were given at birth gifts of intelligence that enable you to learn much more easily and quickly than Steve. But you waste your gifts. Suppose I gave you a ten-dollar bill. Would you buy a ten-cent candy bar and throw the rest of the money away?"

"No, of course not! We're not that foolish!"

"But do you realize that's about what you're doing with your brains?" I put it bluntly. "You fellows could be superior students and do it easier than most of your classmates—if you stopped wasting your brains. And what's more, you'd enjoy school more."

They got the point. It's not always that easy to put across. But a real sense of stewardship would do wonders to eliminate the waste of talent on every hand.

Inspiration is always a personal concern, closely related to one's self-respect and autonomy. All persons tend to behave in ways consistent with their self-concept. A wholesome sense of stewardship enables the gifted child not only to appraise his gifts aright, but to use them in keeping with his best self.

10

HELP THE GIFTED CHILD FIND TIME TO PLAY

Play is a sacred thing, a divine ordinance, for developing in the child a harmonious and healthy organism, and preparing that organism for the commencement of the work of life.

—J. G. Holland

A POPULAR aphorism which used to be quoted liberally —especially by children—was, "All work and no play make Jack a dull boy." Too much work and little play apparently do more than make Jack (or Jane) a dull child. And the brighter the child, the truer this statement is.

It is a sobering fact that the rate of children's suicides has increased more than 100 per cent in the last ten years, and most of them are our brightest boys and girls who feel that the pressure of living is too great.

The gifted child, especially, is pressured as we expect more and more of him and regiment more and more of his time. I know a very bright young lady who gets home from school shortly after 3:30 P.M. After grabbing a quick bite to eat and perhaps answering a phone call from a classmate who is having some problems with homework, she studies, writes papers, does problems quietly and continually until ten or eleven o'clock, sometimes until midnight. On Saturdays she takes ballet lessons, piano lessons, and tries to catch up on homework or papers. On Sunday she attends church school, and later that day youth fellowship. She rarely has time to play.

This is not an unusual situation. All of her friends do it, and she has been doing it since about the third grade. She is now a sophomore in high school, and, unless something drastic happens to change the situation, she will be similarly burdened until she graduates from college. It is not improbable that she will be in a time-bind all the days of her life. Already she feels uncomfortable and ill at ease when a few free minutes come her way.

Educators and Psychologists Are Concerned

Many educators and psychologists are concerned and troubled by the extreme degree of regimentation and pressure put upon our gifted children by home, school, church, or synagogue. Not long ago a colleague of mine, Professor L. Carroll King of Northwestern University, called this pressurization "a crime against a generation." The National Education Association appointed a special committee to investigate the problem. Ann Isaacs, Editor of *The Gifted Child Quarterly* (Fall, 1966) editorialized, "Pressurizing . . . is pervasive. No avenues are left for escape or even temporary departure. The trouble is that the gifted themselves tend to self-impose pressure on their own time and efforts. If the adults provide still more structuring of their time, are we not denying them freedom for further exploration, creation, and self-evaluation?"

Part of the problem stems from some educational fears and misconceptions. October 4, 1957, was a fateful day in American education as Russia's Sputnik I shook us up as few events ever have. As a result, columnists, free-lance writers, generals, admirals, and other "experts" cried loudly, "Our schools are soft! They are failing to challenge our able children. Too much time is spent on nonessentials."

Soon, large numbers of teachers became alarmed by the complaints they heard and read. Unable to think clearly about what should be done, or how it should be done, they just did more of what they were doing already. A study of homework assignments during this period shows that teachers were assigning more than twice as much as before Sputnik I. Twenty sentences became forty, fifteen math problems became thirty, and so on.

Shortly professors, writers, and publishers prepared and published new texts and other materials which, they said, would bring quality to the schools. Millions of teachers went to institutes and workshops financed by the government and philanthropic foundations. There they learned about the "new math" and "new science" and "new English." Without question, many school subjects were brought up-to-date. This was good. But soon parents and students noticed that the teachers who attended these workshops and institutes now assigned work in merciless quantities.

Quality had been improved, but along with it had come intense pressures on children. Mathematics once for seniors was now for sophomores; even eleventh graders were studying college chemistry and physics. Algebra was introduced to third and fourth graders. Many schools jumped into the "new" studies without adequate background for either teacher or student. What happened to the public school also happened in college. Many courses at the undergraduate level were of the same quantity and quality of courses offered a few years ago at the graduate level.

An era of toughness in learning had arrived.

There is no question but what our children can learn this new content and increased quantity. They are doing it. But what a child can do is not always what he *ought* to do.

Along with the mass of difficult material to be learned came increased pressure to get into the "best" colleges. Children had to learn more and more and still get the good grades needed to enter the good colleges. Teachers had to teach more and more with as many pupils and no more time than before.

But in the end it is the children who suffer most. The effect of all this pressure is inevitable. The only way to cope with more and better learning is to produce longer assignments with more homework. Most of our better students spend more time at night on homework and "outside" reading than they do in their entire daytime sessions at school. One hears constantly, "I'm tired. I never get rested up." "I work till twelve or one o'clock, but I can't use my eyes much longer." A fourth grader summed it up: "My parents don't seem to care how long I must study. And each one of my teachers thinks she is the only one who gives me homework. No one cares if I never have time to play."

Sometimes Parents Compound the Problem

Many parents of these bright youngsters are afraid to ask for a letup. Others feel that this pressure is at least necessary, if not good. Their gifted children have much to offer, they say, and they must make the most of it. Life in the last part of the twentieth century will be a grinding, exacting, deadly business, and these future leaders will have to get used to it. And fear of impending problems with college entrance has crept down to the nursery schools.

A father recently expressed it this way: "I want my son to go to Harvard so he will have a real chance at law and politics. Now to get him into Harvard, he will have to attend a top prep school. In order to enter that prep school he'll have to go to an accredited elementary school, and before that he must go to a choice nursery school. He is three now, and I'm looking for a really good prenursery school so that he'll get his foot on the right rung of the ladder early."

During a recent visit to a book store this writer discovered a shelf of books by several different authors of the general title "Teach Your Baby to Read." And to a degree the brighter infants of two or three can learn to read. But *should* gifted babies learn to read?

I am alarmed by this trend. For one thing, if no other, the muscles which control eye convergence are immature and may be permanently damaged by this strain at so early an age. For another, the emotional strain of trying to please demanding and overanxious parents can damage a child's feeling about school and learning, if not his total emotional outlook on life.

With all seriousness of purpose parents too often tend to encroach upon the already limited free time of their gifted children. Sometimes the intent is to develop recreational skills such as skating, dancing, music, tennis, calisthenics, or reading. Nothing has done more to destroy reading for fun than pressure applied by parents or book reports by teachers. And reading ought to be fun—play—but when it is structured or demanded, it ceases to be fun or play and becomes work.

At other times the intent is to develop social skills or graces. And so children are pushed into parties and dates for which they are not yet ready, the motivating glands not yet mature enough to make such activities with the opposite sex interesting. One more point of pressure is added.

Sometimes the Church and Synagogue Compound the Problem

With the best intentions religious leaders feel a responsibility, too, to train Johnny and Jane in the way they should go. This usually means such activities over the weekend as religious education classes, worship services, masses, fellowships, socials, and clubs of various sorts. Not infrequently the church or synagogue believes that the children for whom they feel responsible *need* such activities to fill in boring (or mischief-producing) time gaps.

Obviously, children of all faiths need religious experience. This is an essential part of the development of the whole person. But why not be honest and call it just that? Do not put the false label of *recreation* or *play* on these activities; you will not fool the gifted child. And, furthermore, it is a rare bright child who finds time hanging heavy on his hands.

Play Is Children's Business

When do gifted children have time to play freely? By playing children develop self-control, self-confidence, motor coordination, and problem-solving techniques; they enjoy success experiences and imaginative and creative thinking. Play for children is not, as it may seem to an adult, aimless activity which would benefit from structuring.

Play is a goal-seeking purposive activity in which the child endlessly rehearses, practices, explores, manipulates, investigates, identifies, interacts with, thinks about, and learns whatever he can manage. In his imaginative play and use of play and play materials, he develops miniature replicas of the adult world. He experiments with play things, and ideas, and words, and sounds, and symbols, as he tries to cope with an often perplexing grownup world.

The same results cannot be accomplished in a parent's, or teacher's, or religious leader's structured situation. This approach flounders in the misconception that children cannot learn on their own. As a matter of fact, children learn best and remember longest what they discover by their own efforts.

Play is the best way a child can learn about self and others. He develops manual dexterity and perception, plus a whole category of skills and abilities we call "learning readiness." This actually is a misnomer; what we mean is a readiness to learn school subjects. He has been learning more than we know long before this.

Above all else, free play helps a child develop healthy attitudes toward school, church or synagogue, and himself. It is not unrealistic to think that deprivation of free play defeats all our efforts for a better education, a more stable personality, and a set of effective moral and spiritual values. Deprivation of free play usually will cause a child to hate school. And if the church or synagogue infringes upon his rare free time, he will develop hostility toward these institutions.

When play seems the most purposeless, the child is orienting himself to his environment, to others, and to himself. In free play he endlessly rehearses what later will become directive in all of his activities. That most important of all developments, his self-concept, grows out of play. He needs above all else success experiences that reinforce his self-concept, his skills, and his values. Free play provides these success experiences as he proceeds at his own rate of development and learning. Structure or direct his play and he no longer learns or develops at his own rate; he now must conform to your rate or fail. There is enough necessary structured living without adding structured play.

If the child had only to master his physical world, or the world of school subjects, his task would be relatively easy. The average child has inherited what he needs for sensory discrimination, neuromuscular control, and learning facts. The gifted child is even better off in these areas. But the immature organism we call a child must be humanized and spiritualized. He must learn to live in our culturally and spiritually symbolic world. He must learn to recognize and respond to the meanings of things, events, and people. This he will do in play—if we permit him to do so by giving him the time and freedom he needs.

Suppose that because of the pressures of school, home, and religious group he is deprived of free play or it is severely limited. What happens to him? We usually define a culturally deprived child as one who, because of poverty or a disadvantaged home and community, is restricted, does not develop the learning, skills and abilities, knowledge and self-concept normally expected of a child. He most likely comes from the hills or the slums.

If he is removed from this restricted and impoverished environment to one that is blessed with cultural, intellectual, and emotional stimulation, he will make remarkable strides forward in mental, emotional, and cultural development. But he never will reach the point he could have reached had he not spent so many years in the poor environment. If he stays too long, he will reach a point where he is past helping.

Not all culturally deprived children come from the city slums or the hills of Appalachia. Some come from Main Street and Knob Hill. No institution can ever teach the skills, attitudes, and values which a child can and ought to learn as he plays—freely.

Strive for a Balanced Schedule

This is not to say that the gifted child should have no homework, lessons, clubs, or church- or synagogue-related activities. The problem appears to be that the brighter a child is, the more we expect of him and the more pressure we put on him. He needs some structured activities, but he also needs some free time to play, usually *more* than most gifted children are getting.

One area where the pressure could be removed materially is homework. No research has ever supported the position that homework, as it is usually assigned, enhances learning even a little bit. On the contrary some studies show that children, especially the gifted, do better without homework. And they are happier and easier to live with.

Several years ago the author was associated with Dr. Walter Barbe, then head of the Department of Special Education at Kent State University, in setting up a number of special classes for gifted children. One stipulation he made was no homework for these able students. This did not exclude a reasonable special project or independent study now and then, but none of the "garden variety" kind of homework. These students thrived.

Observation discloses that very few teachers check the homework turned in. What value is there in writing dozens of papers unless they are checked for errors in grammar, composition, spelling, and the like? Such a procedure will do more to reinforce poor work than to improve it. Many students justly label homework, "boring busywork."

Gifted children (all children, for that matter) can learn more by supervised study in school and independent projects independently chosen. If homework is assigned, it should be in reasonable amounts carefully selected—and checked and returned. If this were done, children could go about their main business, play.

Several things can be done to help take the pressure off the gifted child. Work through local parent-teacher groups, mothers' clubs, civic groups, and service clubs to urge schools to reevaluate their homework policies. You can make allowances for the pressure of homework by reducing your demands on his time. And the church or synagogue can help by reconsidering its demands on his time.

Recently a young lady, after being informed that her church was planning a social for its young people, complained, "Don't they know that we have so many things to do that it is impossible to do them all? I resent having to choose between my school and my church."

She is a very bright child, and she added perceptively: "Perhaps there was a time, and perhaps there are places, when kids needed such activities to fill in wide gaps of boring time. But that's not my case. Why should my church compete with the school for my time? Besides, most of their parties are boringly dull."

Certainly the church and synagogue have a real contribution to make to the gifted child's spiritual development. But would it not be more effective if the activities planned were not in competition in time or content with the schools? Can the church or synagogue compete successfully in the types of activities already structured in the school? Is this their business? If the religious institution concentrates on *its* business, gifted children with their predisposition to things spiritual will respond.

Homework, chores, music lessons, clubs, religious activities— some or all may be a part of the gifted child's life, but in *reasonable* amounts so that he has time to play, time to be a child. He will be a grown-up for a long, long time after he is a child. Let's give childhood back to all children.

OTHER AIDS

Bibliography

Tʜɪs is a selected annotated list of books chosen because of their general excellence and adaptability to the matter
of religious education of the gifted child. They are also books
which are for the most part easily understood by the parent or
teacher who has some responsibility for gifted children. These
books were selected, too, because they are readily available in
good public libraries or through booksellers. As this is written,
there are no books available on the gifted child from the religious viewpoint which I consider to have sufficient merit to be
included in this bibliography.

Abraham, Willard. *Common Sense About Gifted Children.* New
    York: Harper & Brothers, 1958, 266 pp. Just as the title suggests,
    it is an easily understood and sensible book for parents and teach-
    ers of the gifted. It contains an excellent list of identifying char-
    acteristics of gifted children, followed by a number of chapters
    on what to do about them.

Barbe, Walter B., editor. *Psychology and Education of the Gifted.*
    New York: Appleton-Century-Crofts, 1965, 534 pp. A carefully
    selected collection of readings. Included are materials on cre-
    ativity, originality, and nonintellectual factors of giftedness. Also
    presented are historical developments, backgrounds, and measure-
    ments of giftedness. There is a section on encouragement of gifted
    children.

Bower, William Clayton. *Moral and Spiritual Values in Education.*
    Lexington: University of Kentucky Press, 1952, 207 pp. A prac-
    tical and simple treatment of the historical decline of moral and
    spiritual values in American education, plus a method of teaching
    values by means of life situations using what we have learned
    about the psychology of education. The book also abounds with
    illustrations and applications.

Fleming, Robert S., ed. *Curriculum for Today's Boys and Girls.* Columbus: Charles E. Merrill Books, Inc., 1963, 661 pp. A very comprehensive treatment by a variety of authorities of modern educational practices for elementary children, but many of the techniques and ideas should work for adolescents as well. There are excellent chapters on creativity and on discovery as teaching techniques. An excellent source book for teachers of religion if the material is adapted.

Freehill, Maurice F. *Gifted Children.* New York: The Macmillan Company, 1961, 397 pp. This book is particularly strong in identification procedures for the gifted. Also helpful is the discussion of the various methods of education now being used, as well as some curriculum suggestions which could be adapted to religious education.

French, Joseph L. *Educating the Gifted.* New York: Henry Holt & Company, 1959, 555 pp. A collection of carefully selected articles and readings that cover a wide range of topics on gifted children. While it is used as a college text, it is not beyond the understanding of an intelligent parent or teacher. Good background in research, various programs, and evaluation of these programs are provided.

Gallagher, James J. *Teaching the Gifted Child.* Boston: Allyn and Bacon, Inc., 1964, 330 pp. Most of the recent developments concerning the education of gifted children are included. It differs from others in that many of its recommendations are based on research conducted by the author, and a number of specific methods and materials are included to aid the teacher of gifted children.

Getzels, J. W. and Jackson, P. W. *Creativity and Intelligence.* New York: John Wiley and Sons, Inc., 1962. The work of these two men along with that of Torrence (see below) has been most influential in creating a new concept of creativity and its importance in our society.

Jersild, Arthur T. *The Psychology of Adolescence.* New York: The Macmillan Company, 1957, 421 pp. While this book is not a book on gifted children, it is invaluable to anyone who has responsibility for gifted adolescents. The greatest loss to the church occurs in this period of development, and the importance of understanding this group cannot be overemphasized. An unusual fact for a secular book is the religious viewpoint maintained. It also has a particularly complete bibliography.

Morse, William C. and Wingo, G. Max. *Psychology and Teaching.* Chicago: Scott, Foresman and Company, 1962. For those who wish to approach teaching from a child developmental and psychological viewpoint, this book is excellent and very readable.

Strang, Ruth. *Helping Your Gifted Child.* New York: E. P. Dutton Company, 1960, 259 pp. This book was written especially for parents of gifted children and presents a general treatment of the subject in simple language. It is replete with illustrations and has an excellent annotated bibliography.

Sumption, Merle R. and Leucking, Evelyn M. *Education of the Gifted.* New York: The Ronald Press Company, 1960, 478 pp. An excellent general presentation of the subject, which is particularly helpful in identification and guidance of the gifted. The role of the community is discussed, and various educational programs, through college, are considered. The bibliographies at the end of each chapter are of particular value to those who desire depth in their study of the gifted child.

Torrance, Paul E. *Guiding Creative Talents.* Englewood Cliffs, New Jersey: Prentice-Hall, Inc., 1962. One of the influential treatments of the whole area of creativity, its identification and development.

Intelligence Tests

Slossen Intelligence Test. A quick and easy-to-use individual test, 10 to 30 minutes. It has a very wide range, measuring ability from small babies to gifted adults. One of the most economical to use, an entire kit costs only $3.75, with enough forms for 20 individuals; additional forms are quite inexpensive. Slossen Education Publications, 140 Pine Street, East Aurora, New York 14052.

The Quick Test. A picture vocabulary test used with children two years of age and older. Complete and easy-to-understand instructions are supplied. Test takes 3 to 10 minutes to administer and costs $8. Psychological Test Specialists, P.O. Box 1441, Missoula, Montana 59801.

Peabody Picture Vocabulary Test. An untimed individual test which is easily administered and has a wide reputation as a very good intelligence test for children and young people from two-and-a-half to eighteen years of age. It takes about 10 to 15 minutes to give and costs $10. American Guidance Service, 720 Washington Avenue, S.E., Minneapolis, Minnesota 55414.